Drupal Search Engine Optimization

Drive people to your site with this supercharged
guide to Drupal SEO

Ric Shreves

[PACKT] open source *
PUBLISHING   community experience distilled

BIRMINGHAM - MUMBAI

Drupal Search Engine Optimization

First published: September 2012

Production Reference: 1060912

Published by Packt Publishing Ltd.
Livery Place
35 Livery Street
Birmingham B3 2PB, UK.

ISBN 978-1-84951-878-9

www.packtpub.com

Cover Image by Neha Rajappan (neha.rajappan1@gmail.com)

Credits

Author
Ric Shreves

Reviewers
Surendra Mohan
Veturi JV Subramanyeswari

Acquisition Editor
Andrew Duckworth

Lead Technical Editor
Andrew Duckworth

Technical Editor
Veronica Fernandes

Copy Editor
Laxmi Subramanian

Project Coordinator
Vishal Bodwani

Proofreader
Mario Cecere

Indexer
Tejal R. Soni

Graphics
Aditi Gajjar

Production Coordinators
Prachali Bhiwandkar
Shantanu Zagade

Cover Work
Prachali Bhiwandkar

About the Author

Ric Shreves is a Web Applications Consultant and Tech Author. He's been building websites and writing about technology since the mid-90s. He specializes in open source Content Management Systems and has written texts on each of the big three – WordPress, Joomla!, and Drupal.

He is the Founding Partner of Water & Stone, a digital agency that focuses on new media and online marketing. He works with clients on Digital Marketing Strategy and supervises the SEO implementation team. He lives in Bali and divides his time between the island and Singapore.

About the Reviewers

Surendra Mohan is serving as Service Delivery Manager at a well-known software consulting European MNC in India.

After completing BE in 2004 from VTU, Belgaum, in the branch of ISE, he started his career as a Software Engineer with .NET technology. Later he advanced into the area of HR/Recruitment/IT Consulting/Software Development/Web Development via Global Solutions while exploring open source web technologies such as Drupal and Ubercart, handling various roles such as a Programmer, Technical Lead, Project Lead, and Technical Architect, ending up as Service Delivery Manager on Drupal.

Sree (aka **Veturi JV Subramanyeswari**) is currently working as Drupal Architect at a well known software consulting MNC in India. After joining this company she served a few Indian MNCs, many start ups, and R&D sectors in various roles such as Programmer, Tech Lead, and Research Assistant. She has around eight years of working experience in web technologies covering Media and Entertainment, Publishing, Healthcare, Enterprise Architecture, Manufacturing, Public Sector, Defense Communication, and Gaming. She is also a well-known speaker who delivers talks on Drupal, Open Source, PHP, Women in Technology, and so on.

She reviewed other technical books such as Drupal 7 Multi Sites Configuration, Building Powerful and Robust Websites with Drupal 6, Drupal 6 Module development, PHP Team Development, Drupal-6-site-blueprints, Drupal 6 Attachment Views, Drupal E-Commerce with Ubercart 2.x, Drupal 7: First Look, and many more.

I would like to thank my family and friends who supported me in completing my reviews on time with good quality.

www.PacktPub.com

Support files, eBooks, discount offers and more

You might want to visit www.PacktPub.com for support files and downloads related to your book.

Did you know that Packt offers eBook versions of every book published, with PDF and ePub files available? You can upgrade to the eBook version at www.PacktPub.com and as a print book customer, you are entitled to a discount on the eBook copy. Get in touch with us at service@packtpub.com for more details.

At www.PacktPub.com, you can also read a collection of free technical articles, sign up for a range of free newsletters and receive exclusive discounts and offers on Packt books and eBooks.

http://PacktLib.PacktPub.com

Do you need instant solutions to your IT questions? PacktLib is Packt's online digital book library. Here, you can access, read and search across Packt's entire library of books.

Why Subscribe?

- Fully searchable across every book published by Packt
- Copy and paste, print and bookmark content
- On demand and accessible via web browser

Free Access for Packt account holders

If you have an account with Packt at www.PacktPub.com, you can use this to access PacktLib today and view nine entirely free books. Simply use your login credentials for immediate access.

Table of Contents

Preface

Drupal is one of the most popular web content management systems. It powers a number of today's websites and is a solid choice for many businesses that want to create a compelling online presence. On today's Web, when noise and competition are at their highest levels ever, simply having a great site isn't enough. If you want to be competitive online, you have to have an appreciation for search marketing and you need fluency with the skills and strategy behind search engine optimization.

Drupal provides only limited SEO functionality straight out of the box. In this book, we look at how you can create a search engine optimized Drupal site using a combination of the default Drupal tools together with a set of popular extensions for the CMS. We also explore in depth the strategy behind SEO and how to set up and prosecute a successful SEO campaign.

Search marketing is a very competitive area, and one that is constantly changing and evolving. SEO skills are in high demand. Use this book to build a solid foundation in SEO and make your Drupal sites perform to the best of their ability.

What this book covers

Chapter 1, An Introduction to Search Engine Optimization, introduces the key concepts behind search engine optimization, including an explanation of how search engines look at websites together with a glossary of terms in common usage in the SEO world.

Chapter 2, Configuring Drupal's SEO Options, focuses on how to configure Drupal to achieve optimal SEO advantage. Each of the default SEO features is discussed at length, as are server configuration issues.

Chapter 3, Useful Extensions to Enhance SEO, reviews the most popular SEO extensions for the Drupal CMS, then covers the installation and configuration of an example extension.

Chapter 4, Getting Ready for Launch, is concerned with the soft skills behind SEO, that is, keyword analysis, competitor research, and the development of an SEO keyphrase strategy for a site.

Chapter 5, Managing SEO on a Live Site, is concerned with what goes on after the site is launched. The focus is on developing a methodology for continuous improvement, with a look at content strategies, Social Media Optimization, and link building.

What you need for this book

Advanced technical skills are not required, however, the reader should be comfortable administering a Drupal website, and familiar with the installation of extensions and modules.

Who this book is for

This book targets site builders, webmasters, and site owners. Advanced technical skills are not required, though the user should be familiar with administering a Drupal website, including how to install extensions. If you are concerned with how your Drupal site ranks on the search engines, or with generating traffic for your site, then you will find this book very useful. The text presumes no existing specialist knowledge. Basic concepts are explained, as is the thinking behind the approach advocated in this book.

Conventions

In this book, you will find a number of styles of text that distinguish between different kinds of information. Here are some examples of these styles, and an explanation of their meaning.

Code words in text are shown as follows: "The `.htaccess` file is a configuration file for your web server."

New terms and **important words** are shown in bold. Words that you see on the screen, in menus or dialog boxes for example, appear in the text like this: "In the navigation menu on the left select the **Diagnostic** menu".

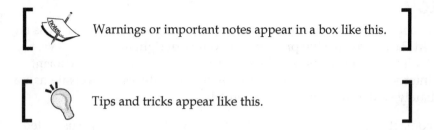

Warnings or important notes appear in a box like this.

Tips and tricks appear like this.

Reader feedback

Feedback from our readers is always welcome. Let us know what you think about this book—what you liked or may have disliked. Reader feedback is important for us to develop titles that you really get the most out of.

To send us general feedback, simply send an e-mail to feedback@packtpub.com, and mention the book title via the subject of your message.

If there is a topic that you have expertise in and you are interested in either writing or contributing to a book, see our author guide on www.packtpub.com/authors.

Customer support

Now that you are the proud owner of a Packt book, we have a number of things to help you to get the most from your purchase.

Errata

Although we have taken every care to ensure the accuracy of our content, mistakes do happen. If you find a mistake in one of our books—maybe a mistake in the text or the code—we would be grateful if you would report this to us. By doing so, you can save other readers from frustration and help us improve subsequent versions of this book. If you find any errata, please report them by visiting http://www.packtpub.com/support, selecting your book, clicking on the **errata submission form** link, and entering the details of your errata. Once your errata are verified, your submission will be accepted and the errata will be uploaded on our website, or added to any list of existing errata, under the Errata section of that title. Any existing errata can be viewed by selecting your title from http://www.packtpub.com/support.

Piracy

Piracy of copyright material on the Internet is an ongoing problem across all media. At Packt, we take the protection of our copyright and licenses very seriously. If you come across any illegal copies of our works, in any form, on the Internet, please provide us with the location address or website name immediately so that we can pursue a remedy.

Please contact us at copyright@packtpub.com with a link to the suspected pirated material.

We appreciate your help in protecting our authors, and our ability to bring you valuable content.

Questions

You can contact us at questions@packtpub.com if you are having a problem with any aspect of the book, and we will do our best to address it.

1
An Introduction to Search Engine Optimization

This chapter lays the foundation for what's to come later in the book. It introduces basic concepts, terms, and fundamental information needed to understand the rationale behind the techniques discussed in the subsequent chapters. While some of the content in this chapter will be known to experienced users, it will be essential content for newbies and those who are not SEO specialists.

The topics covered in this chapter include:

- An introduction to the SEO process
- An SEO vocabulary
- An explanation of how search engines view your site

What is SEO?

At its most basic, SEO is an acronym for Search Engine Optimization. More importantly, for the purposes of the philosophy espoused in this text, SEO is a process — a series of planning and execution steps that lead to a website being optimized to perform its best on the search engines.

Notice the emphasis on process — SEO is not something you do once and then forget about. While an intensive period of attention to your site's optimization factors can lay a solid foundation and get you off to a proper start, if you do not continue to make efforts to improve and respond to market conditions, your rankings will stagnate and then erode over time. Moreover, your efforts do not exist in isolation; there are others out there competing for rankings and traffic. In order to succeed, you need to do your best to stay ahead of the others fighting for ranking for their sites.

[When we talk about the search engines in this text, we mean Google, Bing, Baidu, or other similar sites focused on allowing the general public to search for and find information on the Web. Typically, what works for one search engine will work for others. Though there are peculiarities and optimization strategies that can be applied to target-specific engines, most SEO techniques are search-engine agnostic.]

The competition for attention online should never be underestimated. If you are in a competitive business vertical—be it travel, finance, gambling, web design, property, or others—the battle for traffic from the search engines is cutthroat. Never forget that the major players out there have dedicated SEO teams that do nothing every day but tweak, optimize, build links, create content, and generally do their best to out-compete all other similar business vying for the top spots on the search engines.

In this book, we put forward a methodology for search engine optimization. The process we advocate can be viewed broadly as having two parts—foundations and on-going efforts. We start by looking at how to lay a great foundation for your site, that is, the basics of creating a search engine friendly site. In later chapters, we turn our attention to on-going techniques for maintaining and improving your rankings over time. Along the way, we look at how to formulate and implement a coherent search engine strategy.

[Never forget, for most site owners the actual goal is traffic generation, not pure search engine ranking.]

While many of the issues in SEO relate to technical aspects of the site, there is much more to SEO than just getting the technical aspects of your Joomla! site in order. One of the fundamental principles advocated in this book is to focus on the creation of useful, unique content. There is a strong, positive correlation between high quality content and high site ranking. This is one of the few areas where the search engines provide specific guidance about what they are looking for in a site. On the subject of quality, Google provides the following guidance:

- Make pages primarily for users, not for search engines. Don't deceive your users or present different content to search engines than you display to users, which is commonly referred to as "cloaking".

- Avoid tricks intended to improve search engine rankings. A good rule of thumb is whether you'd feel comfortable explaining what you've done to a website that competes with you. Another useful test is to ask, "Does this help my users? Would I do this if search engines didn't exist?"

For more insights from Google, visit `http://support.google.com/webmasters/bin/answer.py?hl=en&answer=35769`.

Bing also emphasizes the importance of content and advises as follows:

- Ensure content is built based on keyword research to match content to what users are searching for
- Produce deep, content-rich pages; be an authority for users by producing excellent content
- Set a schedule and produce new content frequently
- Be sure content is unique—don't reuse content from other sources

 Don't try to outsmart Google—it's not going to work. Even if you find a way to artificially manipulate your rankings, there will come a day—very soon—when Google will pick up on it and make adjustments to their algorithms. When that happens, your site rankings will plummet and you will go from hero to zero.

While content is critical, it should not be your only concern. SEO practitioners often disagree about the relative importance of various factors in site rankings, but there is general agreement on which factors play a part. The search engine business is very competitive and companies such as Google and Bing do not disclose details of how their algorithms work. Fortunately for us, there is a considerable body of third-party research focused on discerning trends and patterns in search engine ranking. One of the best sources of information on this topic is SeoMoz's Search Ranking Factors, a report they publish free of charge and update annually. The data in the report comes from interviews of more than 130 SEO specialists and from a large data set that seeks to identify correlations between site variables and search engine rank.

 View the report online by visiting `http://www.seomoz.orq/article/search-ranking-factors`.

Among the factors that are agreed to be significant are:

- Keywords in the domain name
- Keywords in a page's URL
- Keywords in the content title
- Keyword placement on page
- Keyword repetition on page

- Uniqueness of content
- Freshness of content
- Facebook activity
- Twitter activity, including influence of account tweeting
- Google+ activity
- Social media up votes and comments
- Click through rate for the site
- Bounce rate for the site
- Number, quality, and content of links to this site
- Number of internal links
- Number of errors on site
- Speed of the site

In sum, SEO is a process that requires a multifaceted strategy. At a minimum, you need to make an effort to create a site that is search engine friendly, but in order for your site to excel in the rankings, you must do more. SEO requires concerted effort across time and you must also focus on the creation of unique, quality content.

The future of SEO

SEO is a moving target. The search engines are constantly adjusting their algorithms and practitioners are constantly trying new strategies and modifying their approach. While it is impossible to predict with any accuracy what the future of SEO will bring, there is some consensus among experts about which direction it is moving in. Generally speaking, we believe the future will see a continued emphasis on determining the perceived value of each site. This will be done by looking at not only the quality of the site's content, but also social media signals and site traffic patterns. Site performance will also continue to be a factor, with faster, better built sites being preferred over slow, badly engineered sites.

These factors are consistent with what we know about the general goals the search engines aspire to, that is, to be able to perceive sites more like users perceive them, rather than as a purely mathematical exercise.

SEO terminology

The SEO field is replete with esoteric terminology and peculiar expressions. An awareness of the discipline's vocabulary is essential to clear understanding. In this section of the chapter, we provide definitions for the most commonly-used terms.

.htaccess

The .htaccess file is a configuration file for your web server. In the context of SEO, it is used to help your web server determine how to route HTTP traffic. In the world of SEO, the .htaccess file is most commonly discussed in the context of URL aliases, which are often used to create search engine friendly URLs.

 Note that .htaccess is only applicable to sites running on the Apache web server. The web.config file performs the same tasks on IIS.

301 redirect (also known as Permanent Redirect)

A 301 redirect is an instruction given to the web server, informing it that a page that was previously located at one URL has been moved permanently to a new URL. The 301 redirect is most commonly used in situations where a site has been rebuilt and the URLs have changed. By adding 301 redirects to the site, you are able to avoid missed connections caused by traffic going to the old URL. When a 301 redirect is used, the search engines will also update their indexes to remove the old URL for the page and substitute the new one, thereby preserving the page's indexing.

302 redirect (also known as Temporary Redirect or Found)

A 302 redirect, like a 301 redirect, informs the web server that a page has moved. Unlike a 301 redirect, a 302 redirect indicates that the move is temporary. This option is a disfavored option as some search engines will penalize for the use of this sort of redirect.

404 error (also known as Page Not Found)

When a person visits a URL to a page that no longer exists (or has been moved), or types in an incorrect URL, the visitor will automatically be shown a 404 error message. The default message informs the visitor that the page cannot be found. Many sites build custom pages specifically designed to be displayed when a 404 error occurs.

AdSense

AdSense is a Google advertising program aimed at website owners. Site owners can sign up for the AdSense program and then display it on their site. (The ad inventory is provided by Google, often from the AdWords program, discussed next). The website owner will be paid a percentage of the revenues generated when someone clicks on one of the ads displayed on his or her site.

AdWords

AdWords is a Google commercial advertising program aimed at advertisers. If you want to advertise on the Google network, you can sign up for the AdWords program, build an ad and set a daily budget for the display of that ad. The ad will then appear in the Google network and you will be charged when someone clicks on one of the ads (or, alternatively, you can elect to be charged according to the number of views of the ad).

Alexa Rank

`Alexa.com` provides a website ranking service that attempts to rate all the sites on the Web in order of their popularity. Like a golf score, the lower the score, the better. The most popular site on the Web (typically `Google.com`) has an Alexa Rank of 1. The service, though not 100 percent accurate and the subject of some criticism, is yet another way of tracking the success of your efforts to raise your site's profile. To learn more visit `http://alexa.com`.

Alt attribute

The HTML image tag (`img`) is used to place images on the page. The tag includes an option to specify a value for the attribute `alt`. This attribute is intended to allow webmasters to specify an alternative description for the image, typically for the benefit of users who are using screen readers or browsers with the image display disabled.

Anchor

Anchors are hyperlinks that allow a user to jump from one place to another within the same page.

Back link (also known as an "inbound link")

A back link is a link on an external site that points to your site.

Bing Webmaster

The Bing Webmaster service is provided by Microsoft to enable site owners to gain access to some basic tools that help you diagnose and track your site. Registration is free of charge.

Black hat

Black hat is a label used to describe the use of SEO techniques that are illegal, unethical, or of questionable propriety.

Bot (also known as Robot, Spider, or Crawler)

A robot, or "bot" for short, is a software agent that indexes web pages. It is also called a "spider" or a "crawler".

Canonical URLs

Canonical URLs are URLs that have been standardized into a consistent form. For the search engines, this typically implies making sure all your pages use consistent URL structures, for example, making sure all your URLs start with "www".

Cloaking

Cloaking is a black hat SEO technique that involves presenting the search engine spider with different content than you show a normal site visitor.

Crawl depth

Crawl depth is a measure of how deeply the search engine spider has indexed a website. This is typically an issue relevant for sites with a complex hierarchy of pages. The deeper the spider indexes the site, the better.

Deep link

Deep link is a hyperlink that points to something other than the front page of a website.

Doorway page (also known as a "gateway page")

Doorway page is a page built specifically to point users to another page. This technique is used legitimately when a site owner holds multiple domain names and wishes to channel all the traffic into a primary domain. The technique is often used inappropriately by some black hat SEO practitioners as a way to create highly optimized pages targeting a specific term or terms, then push the users to another site—an online variation of the old bait and switch routine.

Duplicate content penalty

Duplicate content penalty is a theory that the search engines penalize sites that repeat content, or use content that is duplicated from another source. The theory is controversial, with many believing that the penalty may not exist, or may only be enforced in situations where there are other factors that indicate bad intent.

Google Webmaster

The Google Webmaster service is provided by Google to enable site owners to gain access to some basic tools that help you diagnose and track your site. Registration is free of charge.

Internal link density

Internal link density is the number of self-referential links on a site; that is, the number of links on a site pointing to other pages on the same site.

KEI

KEI is an acronym standing for Keyphrase Effectiveness Index. KEI is normally used during keyphrase research in an attempt to find the optimal keyphrases for a site. It is a simple ratio, most often defined as, "Frequency of search engine queries for the term/number of pages competing for the term".

More the number of searches, more the potential traffic. The lower the competition, the easier it is to rank highly in the SERP. The most ideal term will have low competition and a high number of searches.

Keyphrase density (also known as "keyword density")

Keyphrase density is a calculation done by looking at all the text on a page, then calculating a ratio that represents the total number of words to the number of times a particular keyphrase or keyword appears on that page.

Keyword (or Keyphrase)

A keyword is a word being targeted for site's SEO efforts. A keyphrase is simply the targeting of a phrase instead of a single word.

Keyphrase stuffing

Keyphrase stuffing is the over-optimizing of a page for a particular keyphrase. This is a disfavored practice that can have a negative impact on your site's ranking as it is viewed by the search engines as an attempt to exert inappropriate influence on the rankings for the page.

Landing page

A landing page is a web page that has been optimized to capture a customer, and is typically used as the target for an ad or other promotional campaign, or simply for capturing leads.

Link building

Link building is the process of seeking out or creating links to a site for the purpose of increasing the site's search engine relevance or inbound traffic.

Link farm

Link farm is a site that includes an excessive number of links. These sites are typically built purely to generate links for SEO purposes. Sites of this nature are disfavored by the search engines, which view them as inappropriate attempts to exert influence over rankings.

Link text (also known as "anchor text")

When you create a hyperlink on a page by wrapping a text string with an `<a>` tag, the text wrapped by the tag is referred to as the link or anchor text. There is a search engine optimization benefit to using text for hyperlinks, as the text can then be indexed in conjunction with the hyperlink.

Long tail

In general terms, the long tail of a distribution is the trailing end of the distribution. In the context of SEO, the term is used to refer to targeting longer and more specific search queries, where there is usually less competition.

Meta tags

Metadata is, quite literally, data about data. On the Web, meta tags are the most common implementation of metadata and in the past were a key part of search engine indexing. Today, meta tags are still in use on the Web and can be found in the head section of web pages.

MozRank

MozRank is a site ranking algorithm formulated by SeoMoz. Often used in SEO circles as an alternative to Google's PageRank.

nofollow

`nofollow` is a possible value for the `rel` attribute inside the `<a>` tag. If the value of the `rel` attribute for a link is set to `nofollow`, the search engines' spiders will not follow or index the link.

Organic rank

Organic rank refers to natural search engine ranking, as opposed to paid ranking.

Outbound link

Outbound link is a hyperlink on one site pointing to an external site.

PageRank

PageRank is a ranking algorithm created by and named for Larry Page at Google. The ranking criteria is unknown, but the scale ranges from zero at the low end to ten at the high end. The higher the score the more persuasive a website is deemed to be. There is argument, however, that the rank is no longer in use at Google and may not continue to evolve.

PPC

PPC is an acronym for Pay Per Click advertising. If you use a PPC advertising scheme, you pay every time someone clicks on one of your ads. The most popular PPC system is the Google AdWords program. It is also sometimes called "pay for performance advertising".

Reciprocal link

Reciprocal link is a link from one site to another, given in exchange for a link back. It is a link exchange between webmasters, done in hopes of boosting both sites' rankings.

Redirect

Redirect is an instruction given to the web server to redirect traffic seeking one URL to a different URL. There are different types of redirects, such as 301 redirect and 302 redirect, as we have seen earlier in this chapter.

Robots.txt

`Robots.txt` is a file containing instructions for search engine robots. This file is located on the server but is not used by the human visitors to the website.

SEF URLs

SEF URLs is an acronym for Search Engine Friendly URLs. The term refers to the creation of URLs that use natural words and phrases, rather than query strings and other abstract values (such as numbers) not associated with the page content.

SEM

SEM is an acronym for Search Engine Marketing. The term is broad and applies to not only search engine optimization, but also to other techniques, such as social media, pay per click advertising, and other marketing techniques focused on search engines.

SEOMoz

SEOMoz is a popular commercial SEO consultancy service. Learn more at `http://www.seomoz.org`.

SERP

SERP is an acronym for Search Engine Results Page.

SMO

SMO is an acronym for Social Media Optimization. The process of using social media to drive traffic to your site and the related process of making your site suitable for social media, for example, by including social bookmarking tools and other social sharing devices on the site's pages.

Splash page

Splash page is an entry page, typically decorative, used to greet visitors to a website.

Stop word

Stop words are words included in search queries that are not actively indexed, unless included in quotations (phrase search). Typical examples include articles and conjunctions such as the, a, and or.

Title attribute

The `title` attribute is available on a number of HTML elements. It is used to provide a description for a link, a table, a frame, an image, or other elements. Some search engines index the `title` attribute and it therefore provides another option for on page optimization. Some browsers will also display the content of the `title` attribute as a tool tip when you move your mouse over the object.

White hat

White hat is a label used to describe the use of SEO techniques that are legal, ethical, or exhibit best practices.

XML sitemap

XML sitemaps lists the pages on a website in a format that is easily digestible by search engine agents. The sitemaps follow a standard convention agreed upon by all the major search engines. The XML sitemap is typically not visible to site visitors, and should not be confused with the normal sitemaps often used on the frontend of websites.

How search engines assess sites?

Search engines all function in approximately the same fashion—a software agent, known as a bot, spider, or crawler, visits a page, gathers the content, and stores it in the search engine's data repository. Once the information is in the repository, it is indexed. The crawling and indexing processes are constant and on-going. Each of the major search engines maintain multiple crawlers that work tirelessly to refresh their index. The spiders find new pages by a variety of methods, typically including XML sitemaps, URLs already in the index, links to pages discovered while indexing, and URLs submitted for inclusion by users. How frequently they visit a specific site, and how deeply they spider the site on each visit, varies.

When a user visits the search engine and runs a search, the search engine extracts (from the search engine's index) a list of pages that are relevant to the query and then displays that list of pages to the user. The output on the search results page is defined according to each search engine's own criteria. The ranking methodology used by each engine is the result of the search engine's secret algorithm.

The search engine's crawler is primarily interested in certain types of information on the page, particularly the URL, the text, and the links on the page. Formatting is not indexed. Images and other media are indexed by most search engines, but to varying degrees of depth. Some types of media, such as Flash or attached files, are rarely indexed, though there are exceptions.

Seeing what the spider sees

If you have a Google Webmaster account, you can see a web page exactly as the Googlebot (the name of the Google crawler) sees it. To do this, log in to Google Webmaster Tools (`http://www.google.com/webmasters/`) and click on a site profile. In the navigation menu on the left, select the **Diagnostics** menu and then select the option **Fetch as Googlebot**. Type the URL of the page you want to see and after a delay, the system will produce the results. You can see a webpage, as shown in the following screenshot, followed by the Googlebot's view of the same page:

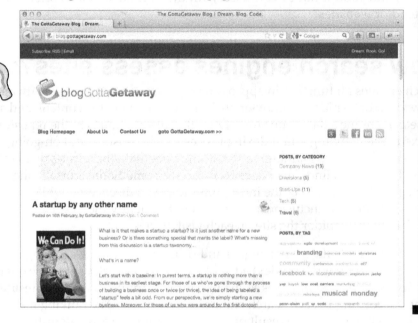

The following is the spider's view of the same page:

Summary

This chapter seeks to acquaint you with the basic principles of search engine optimization, including the terminology used. As noted at the outset, the philosophy that is promoted in this book emphasizes SEO as an on-going process intended to optimize a website to perform its best on the search engines. Throughout this book, the techniques discussed will all reinforce this process-oriented approach to SEO.

At the conclusion of this chapter, you should have gained an awareness of the most commonly used terms in the SEO field and you should have also gained insights into what is indexed by the search engines and how it is used to produce search engine results. At the outset of this chapter we stated the importance of quality and original content; at the end of this chapter, where we provided an example of how a search engine spider views your page, you can once again see how the content is key to your efforts.

In the next chapter, we take our first steps towards laying the foundations of SEO for your site, as we look at the default SEO options that are available on your Drupal site.

2
Configuring Drupal's SEO Options

Out of the box, the Drupal system includes a number of options that can be configured to provide a basic search engine friendly site and lay the groundwork for your on-going SEO efforts. In this chapter we look at the default options, what they mean, and how to optimize them. While the default SEO options in Drupal provide you with basic features you need, such as search engine friendly URLs, this is just the beginning of what you can—and should—do to optimize your site effectively.

The topics covered in this chapter include:

- Configuring your Site Details
- Creating basic search engine friendly URLs
- Optimizing URL aliases
- Controlling taxonomy and tagging
- Setting up your site's RSS feed

Configuring Site Details

Let's start by looking at one of the simplest elements in your site setup, configuring Drupal's **Site Details**. The **Site Details** section of the **Configuration** manager includes three items that are of interest for SEO:

- Site name
- Slogan
- Error pages

We will now discuss each of these in brief.

Setting the site name

You get your first chance to give your site a name during the Drupal installation process. Once the installation is complete, however, you can modify the site name at any time via the **Configuration** manager. The site name is the key to you for several reasons:

- It automatically appears on the site header in many themes, as highlighted in the following screenshot
- It appears as the page title shown in the top browser bar and browser tab, as highlighted in the following screenshot
- If a browser supports tabs, the name will also appear on the browser tab for the page
- The name appears in e-mails generated by the system

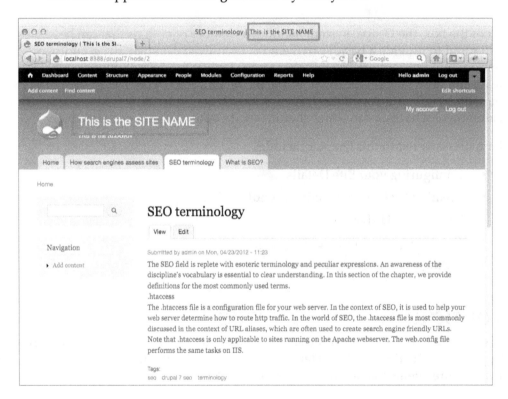

From an SEO perspective, the site name is the key due to its usage in the page title tag. The page title tag is shown on the SERP listing for your page. Accordingly, you want to make sure that the name you select respects your brand and if possible, helps reinforce your keyphrase strategy. Both the search engines and the users look to the site title tag for information about the nature and identity of your site.

To modify the site name, follow the given steps:

1. Access the admin dashboard of your Drupal site.
2. Click on the **Configuration** link on the admin navigation menu at the top of the page.
3. In the **System** section of the page, click on the link labeled **Site information**.
4. Enter the text you want to use in the field marked **Site name**.
5. Click on the **Save configuration** button.

Setting the slogan

Drupal offers the option for the site administrator to specify a slogan for the site. The slogan appears in the following situations:

- Underneath the site name, or logo, in many themes, as highlighted in the following screenshot.

- As part of the page title on the home page (only) of the site, as highlighted in the following screenshot:

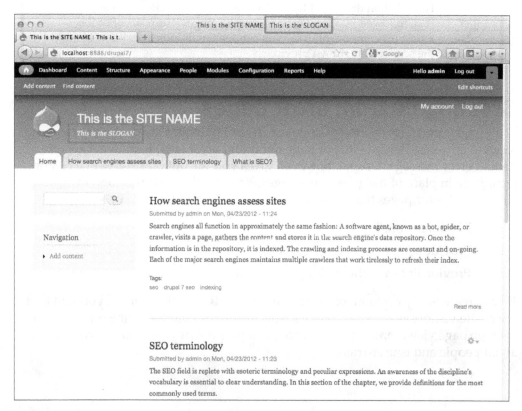

The slogan presents you with another chance to display your primary keyphrases in a prominent position and to get them into the page title of the home page. Accordingly, it's worth using this field to advance your SEO goals.

 In *Chapter 3, Useful Extensions to Enhance SEO*, we also discuss extensions that can be used to enhance your management of the title tag.

To add a slogan to your site, follow the given steps:

1. Access the admin dashboard of your Drupal site.
2. Click on the **Configuration** link on the admin navigation menu at the top of the page.
3. In the **System** section of the page, click on the link labeled **Site information**.
4. Enter the text you want to use in the field marked **Slogan**.
5. Click on the **Save configuration** button.

 Note that on the page title for the home page, the site name appears first, followed by the slogan; on internal pages it appears after the article (or component) title. You can see the different positions in both the screenshots shown previously.

Creating custom error pages

Error pages are an issue often overlooked in SEO planning. By default, a user who receives an access denied (403) or page not found error (404) is shown a generic, default error message. Drupal, however, gives you the option to present a custom error page in place of the generic messages. You should use this option to create customized error pages that achieve all, or part, of the following goals:

- Reinforce your brand
- Provide a friendly error message
- Provide links to other valid pages in your site

If you create nicely customized error pages that advance these goals, you will lose fewer site visitors as a result of errors. This improves your user time on site, your average page views, and helps advance perceptions that your brand is concerned about people and is user-friendly.

To set up custom error pages, follow the given steps:

1. Access the admin dashboard of your Drupal site.
2. Create a new Drupal content page to be used for the error page. Publish it and note the URL.
3. Click on the **Configuration** link on the admin navigation menu at the top of the page.
4. In the **System** section of the page, click on the link labeled **Site information**.
5. Scroll down to the bottom of the page and find the section named **Error Pages**.
6. Enter the relative path to the custom error page in the fields provided.
7. Click on the **Save configuration** button.

Now, when a user is displayed with a 403 or 404 error, they will see your customized error page rather than a generic error message. The following screenshot shows one example of this technique; in this case, we've created a friendly page that will display when a 404 error occurs. Note that we've added links to guide the user and keep them on the site.

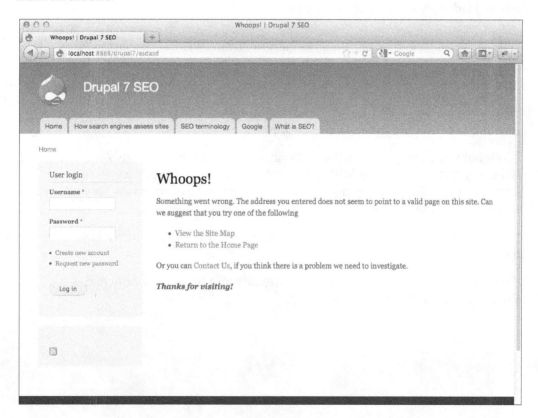

Setting up search engine friendly URLs

We now go from one of the most basic tasks to one of the most important—setting up **search engine friendly (SEF)** URLs. Let's start the discussion by setting a clear definition of what it means for a site to have search engine friendly URLs.

Sites created with content management systems such as Drupal, rely on interaction with the database for the display of content. Accordingly, the URLs often include query strings and other characters that are needed to extract that data from the database. (In contrast, a simple HTML site doesn't have this issue; as a result, its URLs are typically much simpler and lack the complexity seen in CMS-powered websites).

URLs containing query strings and other odd characters are hard for both humans and search engines to read. Ideal URLs are readable and tell us something about the content of the page. By default, the Drupal system produces complex URLs containing additional characters that serve no useful purpose for the site visitor. Accordingly, your first step towards making Drupal more search engine friendly is to get rid of the messy URLs and replace them with SEF URLs. Let's look at two real examples drawn from the default Drupal installation (with some sample content loaded) to contrast the differences.

 Note that Drupal prefers the term "clean URLs", as opposed to the label we use here, that is, "search engine friendly URLs". The terms, however, are interchangeable.

The Drupal system, with no additional configuration, produces a URL that looks something like `http://www.yoursite.com/?q=node/2`.

That is not search engine friendly. Not only is it hard to read, but also the odd characters and query strings will cause problems with some search engines. Moreover, the URL is simply not human friendly; it is hard to remember and even harder to type accurately.

However, with a bit of configuration, you can get Drupal to produce a URL that looks something like `http://www.yoursite.com/how-search-engines-work`.

The previous URL is both search engine friendly and human friendly and is superior for both reasons.

Drupal provides two levels of support for the creation of search engine friendly URLs. The most basic level simply removes the query strings. A second, more advanced option is custom URL rewriting, which allows you to create fully customized URLs. The previous example shows a fully customized URL resulting from the site administrator both enabling Drupal's **Clean URLs** option and writing a URL alias for the content item.

Everything you need to create optimal SEF URLs is included in your default Drupal installation. Two different Drupal features combine to produce the result we saw in the previous example—Clean URLs and the Path module. In Drupal 7, the automatic installer will try to enable both of these features for you at the time the site is installed. In most cases, you should not need to do anything else (except of course write any custom URL aliases you want).

 By default, with Clean URLs and the Path Module enabled, Drupal will automatically create a URL alias out of the title of a content item. You can, however, modify this to suit your own preferences. Creating custom URL aliases is discussed later in this chapter.

Enabling Clean URLs

Let's look at how to enable both features, just in case they were not enabled at installation, or in case someone has disabled those features on your site after the installation was completed. First, to enable the Clean URLs feature of Drupal, follow the given steps:

1. Access the admin dashboard of your Drupal site.
2. Click on the **Configuration** link on the admin navigation menu at the top of the page.
3. Find the section named **Search and Metadata**, and then select the option **Clean URLs**.
4. If your server and installation are able to run Clean URLs, you should see the screen shown in the following screenshot. If you see this, simply click on the **Enable clean URLs** checkbox.

5. Click on the **Save configuration** button and you should be greeted by a confirmation dialogue.

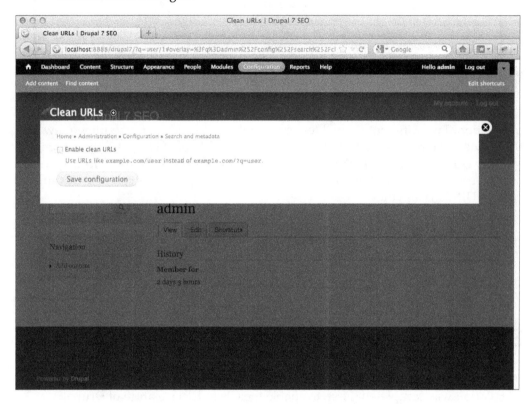

If there is an issue blocking the use of Clean URLs, you will not see the previous screen, but rather a different dialogue, informing you that there is a problem and directing you to an online help file. That screen will also contain a button labeled **Run the clean URL test**. You can click on that button to confirm whether there is a problem. If the issue remains, it is likely that your server is not set up to permit the use of Clean URLs and you will need to read the online help files and possibly also contact your webhost or server administrator.

 The online help files for the Clean URLs feature can be found at http://drupal.org/node/15365.

Another possible problem, though very rare, is that the .htaccess file included with your Drupal installation is missing or flawed. By default, Drupal comes with a .htaccess file; it should be located in the root of the installation. Check your site to make sure it is there and that is has not been modified in such a fashion as to defeat its ability to function properly.

Enabling the Path module

With the **Search Engine Friendly URLs** option enabled, you will have basic SEF URLs for your site. However, if possible, you will want to do more. URL rewriting will allow you to control the URL contents by manually specifying the alias, rather than relying on the system to create them automatically.

The URL rewriting function in Drupal is powered by the Path module. As noted earlier, this should have been enabled automatically during installation, but if it was not, or has been disabled, you can easily turn it back on by following the given steps:

1. Access the admin dashboard of your Drupal site.
2. Click on the **Modules** link on the admin navigation menu at the top of the page.
3. Scroll down the list of modules until you find the module named **Path**.
4. If it is not already selected, click on the checkbox next to the module name.
5. Click on the **Save configuration** button.

Writing Custom URL aliases

The URL for your content items is a key factor in your SEO efforts. It's generally agreed among SEO practitioners that keywords in your URL are influential on the way search engines view that content item. Accordingly, you want to make an effort to use the URL as a way to advance your SEO goals.

Drupal's Path module provides you with enhanced ability to create more search engine effective URLs. Assuming you have set your Drupal site to use Clean URLs and that the Path module is active, as described previously, Drupal will automatically create URL aliases for your content items. The automatic aliases, however, are based on the article's title, and may not always be optimal. While the default aliases may be fine for some sites, if you are concerned about competitive SEO you will want to exercise your own control over the aliases. Fortunately, Drupal makes it possible for you to specify your own URL aliases.

 In the next chapter, we look at a module that lets you create customized automation of URL aliases, giving you improved functionality.

The URL alias for a content item can be manually specified either at the time the item is created or at any time later. To set the alias at the time of content creation, simply scroll down to the bottom of the content editing screen and look for the tab labeled **URL path settings**. Click on that tab and then enter your desired alias in the text field provided.

Note that you need to enter a relative path in the textbox and don't add a trailing slash, else the URL alias will not work.

If you wish to modify a URL alias after a content item has been created, you have two options—either edit the content item, as per the explanation immediately above, or use the URL aliases option provided in the Drupal configuration dashboard.

 The URL aliases screen makes it easy to see all the aliases in one place.

To use this option, follow the given steps:

1. Access the admin dashboard of your Drupal site.
2. Click on the **Configuration** link on the admin navigation menu at the top of the page.
3. Find the section named **Search and Metadata**, and then select the option **URL aliases**.
4. On the URL aliases screen, you will see a list of all the aliases in the system. Find the one you wish to modify and click the **edit** link to the right of the alias.
5. On the screen that loads, type your preferred alias for the item into the **Path alias** field.
6. Click on the **Save** button.

 It's best to set your aliases at the time you publish the page. If you change the alias subsequent to the publication of the item, you run the risk of breaking links to the existing page and creating errors. If you must change the alias after the page has gone live, you will want to create a 301 redirect to make sure that you do not lose traffic to the page or indexing of that page on the search engines.

Setting up taxonomy and tagging

Drupal comes bundled with a content tagging functionality. The system allows you to create tags either before, or during, content creation and associate those terms with content items. The tags can also be grouped together into "vocabularies".

Tagging provides a useful way for your site visitors to discover and access related content. Tags also create useful SEO opportunities; use them to add keyphrases and related concepts to your content items. Going further, in Drupal, it's easy to create menu items from your tags, allowing you to build pages that contain all the content items that have been tagged with a particular term. When you combine the ability to create tag pages with the functionality of the path module, you wind up with a great way to produce URLs and content pages that solidly reinforce your keyphrases strategy.

Though it is a bit outside the scope of this book, note that you can edit your content types to force users to select tags from a specific vocabulary when they create content items. To learn how to modify the content item field settings, visit the official Drupal documentation at http://drupal.org/documentation/modules/field-ui.

By way of example, let's set up a keyphrase optimized page using features from Drupal's taxonomy and path modules. In this example, we'll create a new vocabulary, add some terms to it, set an SEO-optimized URL alias, then create a menu item that points to the tag.

First, let's create a new vocabulary to hold the terms we want to feature by following the given steps:

1. Access the admin dashboard of your Drupal site.
2. Click on the **Structure** link on the admin navigation menu at the top of the page.
3. Select the option **Taxonomy**.
4. You are now in the Taxonomy manager. Click on the **Add vocabulary** link.
5. Let's make a new vocabulary called "search engines". Type search engines in the **Name** field. Add a description in the **Description** field if you like (this is optional).
6. Click on the **Save** button.

Creating new vocabularies is optional; we include it here simply to demonstrate how it is done. If you want, you can always just use the default vocabulary called "tags" to hold all your terms. Generally speaking, adding new vocabularies is most helpful when you either have large number of tags or when you wish to create nested hierarchies of tags.

Next, let's add some terms to our new vocabulary. Follow the given steps:

1. On the Taxonomy manager page, click on the **add terms** link to the right of the vocabulary **search engines**.

2. Type Google in the **Name** field. Add a description in the **Description** field if you like; this is optional.

3. In the **URL alias** field type searchengines/google—this will be our URL for the page containing all content items tagged with this term. Refer to the following screenshot to see how we did this.

4. Click on the **Save** button.

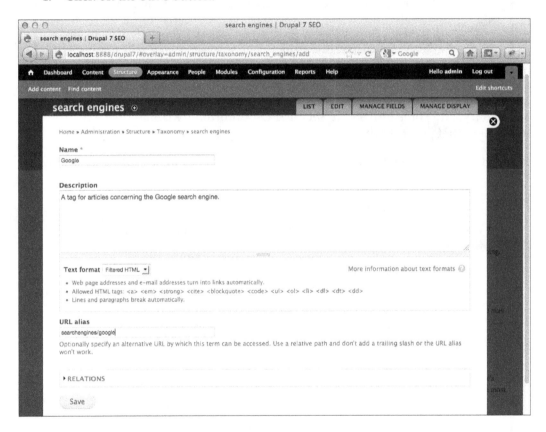

Finally, to complete this task, let's add a menu item to our site to direct users to this new page and expose it better for search engine indexing. Follow the given steps:

1. Click the **Structure** link on the main admin navigation menu.

2. Select the option **Menus**.

3. The Menu manager will load in your browser. Select the **add link** option next to the **Main menu**.

4. Give a name to the menu item by typing in the **Menu link title** field. For this example, let's use `Google`.

5. For the **Path** field, type in the URL we gave to the tag when we created it in the previous steps.

6. Click on the **Save** button.

The task is complete. You now have a new vocabulary, a new tag, and a new menu item. Moreover, the new menu item has a nicely optimized URL string (assuming our SEO strategy is to promote content focused on Google and the search engines!). As you create new content items and tag them with the term Google, the items will automatically be listed on the page connected to the menu item.

Controlling the title attribute on menu items

When you add or edit a menu item, you are given the ability to add a description to the item. The information in the description field is used by Drupal as the title attribute for the menu item. That means the text will show up as a tool tip when users move their mouse over the menu link. The title attribute is primarily intended to be of aid to users with accessibility issues. The text, therefore, should be helpful to users in accurately describing the contents of the link. The title attribute also presents another opportunity for you to enhance your own page SEO by including in that description field your target keyphrases or related concepts. Do not, however, use it as an additional way to simply pack a bunch of keywords into your page—that runs contrary to the purpose of the title attribute and is not an appropriate usage of this feature. Use the description field to write a brief description of the target page, but do it in a fashion consistent with your SEO goals.

Configuring your site's RSS feeds

RSS feeds are an effective way of exposing your site's content both to users and to the various indexing services. Drupal comes with RSS capabilities; you don't need to add any extensions to publish your site's content via RSS. You do, however, need to configure the feed and add the subscription link to your site.

There are two steps to the task we need to complete. First, we need to configure the RSS feed, then we need to add a link to the feed on our site's pages.

To set up the feed, follow the given steps:

1. Access the admin dashboard of your Drupal site.
2. Click on the **Configuration** link on the admin navigation menu at the top of the page.
3. Find the **Web Services** section of the page and select the option **RSS publishing**.
4. Enter some descriptive text in the **Feed description** field. Make sure you keep your keyphrase strategy in mind here, but also make sure it is user-friendly and useful.
5. Set the **Feed content** combobox to **Title plus teaser**. This will encourage readers to come back to your site to read the full article.
6. Click on the **Save configuration** button.

Next, we want to display the RSS syndication button on your site so that users can discover, and hopefully subscribe to, your site's feed. Drupal makes it easy to add in the button. The system includes, by default, a block named **Syndicate**. The block is unpublished by default. To display the block on your theme, follow the given steps:

1. Access the admin dashboard of your Drupal site.
2. Click on the **Structure** link on the admin navigation menu at the top of the page.
3. Click on the option **Blocks** and the Block manager will load in your browser.
4. Scroll down the page until you find the block named **Syndicate**.
5. From the **Region** combobox, select the name of the region where you want the block to appear.
6. Click on the **Save blocks** button.

The standard RSS icon will now appear on the site, as you can see highlighted in the left column on the page in the following screenshot:

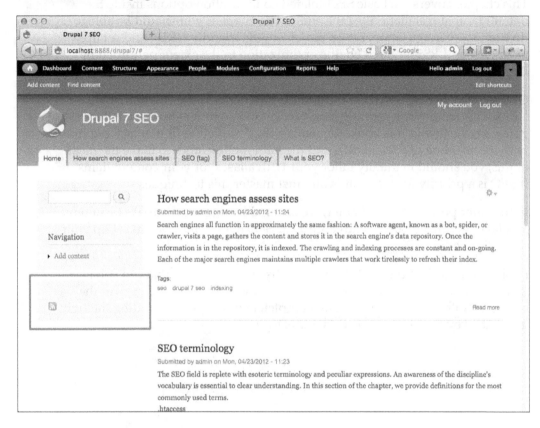

 Note that in the previous screenshot, we have hidden the block title. The block title visibility can be controlled by clicking on the **configure** link next to the block's name in the Block manager.

Summary

This chapter covers the basic SEO-related configuration options inside the default Drupal installation. At the end of this chapter, you should be able to do basic site configuration, set up search engine friendly URLs, and set up taxonomy and RSS—search engine optimization to the extent permitted by the default Drupal system.

Of the concepts discussed, the most important by far is the creation of SEF URLs. This feature is a necessity and you should complete this task before going any further in this book. Remember the completion of that task requires both the enabling of Clean URLs and the Path module and, to make the most of this, you should manually tailor your URL aliases for your content items. If SEO is a priority for your site, you must master this technique.

In the latter portion of the chapter, we covered how to use Drupal's taxonomy and tagging functionality to advance your SEO efforts and how to set up your site's RSS feeds.

Looking forward, in the next chapter we discuss extensions that can enhance your SEO efforts. Some of these extensions provide improvements over the basic system's functions, others add completely new options. Finding the right mix is the key to your SEO success with Drupal.

3
Useful Extensions to Enhance SEO

One of the clear advantages of the Drupal system is the existence of a large number of extensions that can be plugged in to expand the functionality of the default system. A number of these extensions are designed to enhance your ability to achieve search engine optimization. Like the extensions in other categories, the SEO extensions are of varying functionality and quality. In this chapter, we look at a number of SEO extensions with the goal of helping you understand exactly what they can do and why you might want to consider adding them to your Drupal site. We then look at the configuration of some of the more complex extensions.

Topics covered in this chapter include:

- How to find extensions for your Drupal site
- Our list of the top SEO-related extensions for Drupal 7
- How to install and configure common SEO extensions

 Note that the extensions in this chapter are all compatible with Version 7.x of Drupal; most also offer versions compatible with older Drupal releases.

Finding SEO modules

While you can always visit Google and run a search for Drupal SEO extensions, there's a better way to find modules and components for your Drupal site. The Drupal community maintains a large directory of extensions specifically for the CMS at `http://drupal.org/project/modules`.

The **Download & Extend** section of the official Drupal site is a great starting point for finding useful extensions. For each module, the directory includes a description, bug reports, and information about compatibility. Some listings also include links to demos or screenshots.

At the time this was written, there were more than 4,000 modules available for Version 7 of Drupal. Some modules overlap with others and some require you to install other extensions before you can use them. Accordingly, your first step should be to look at a number of extensions and decide what combination of extensions is most suitable for your site.

Always check carefully the compatibility of the extensions. Modules or themes created for older versions of Drupal are unlikely to work properly with newer versions of the system. The extensions listed in the directory include final production versions as well as alpha, beta, and development releases. Ideally, you want to select final production releases; you should always think twice about installing beta versions—and we strongly recommend against using alpha or dev version on live sites!

To begin your search, simply visit `http://drupal.org`. Look for the search box at the top right of the page. Enter your query and select the **Modules** option below the text field. Once you click on the **Search** button, the site will return a list of search results. To find only those extensions compatible with Drupal 7, simply click on the combo box labeled **Filter by compatibility:** and select the option **7.x**; the system will automatically update the list of results to show you those that are compatible with Version 7 of Drupal.

Top SEO modules for Drupal

The extensions discussed in this chapter take a variety of forms: some are complete components, some are APIs that enable other functionality, and many are combinations of these things all bundled into one. The exact nature of the extension is really of little importance to you as an SEO practitioner. What is important is the functionality the extension delivers.

The modules listed in the following sections provide a range of functionality. Which are right for you is a personal decision. You should always try to avoid installing things that you will not use. That is, you should favor the simpler, more narrowly tailored solutions, which you will regularly utilize. You also need to consider the added overhead that comes from having multiple modules installed on a site. Once the site is deployed, someone will have to maintain the modules and keep them patched and up to date.

 The modules that are listed next are presented in alphabetical order.

Drupal SEO Tools

Drupal SEO Tools (`http://drupal.org/project/seotools`) is different than the other modules on this list in that it is a comprehensive SEO suite. This extension takes an "all-in-one" approach to Drupal SEO, handling research, implementation, and reporting. The module provides a dashboard that integrates Google Analytics reports (and Google Webmaster) with your Drupal modules. At the time this text was written, the Drupal 7 version of this module was still in Alpha—use at your own risk!

 Note this extension has a number of prerequisites that must be installed before use, and an even longer list of recommended modules.

Facebook social plugins integration

The Facebook Social module (`http://drupal.org/project/fb_social`) provides Drupal integration of the full suite of Facebook social plugins, including the like button, comments, recommendations, activity feed, subscribe button, and more. The configuration options also give you the chance to control the URL version submitted to Facebook from your site (assuming of course the users submit the link using the tools provided by this module!).

Global Redirect

Global Redirect (`http://drupal.org/project/globalredirect`) is a utility module that helps preserve the integrity of URL aliases in place on your site. It performs multiple tasks, including canonicalization, assuring that trailing slashes are removed, making sure duplicate content is blocked, checking permissions and access to nodes, and verifying that clean URLs are being implemented properly. The module's role is essentially housekeeping: keeping it clean and avoiding redundancy. See the discussion later in this chapter on configuration.

Meta tags

The default Drupal installation comes without editable metadata fields. You will want to install a module to add this function to your site and the Meta tags module (`http://drupal.org/project/metatag`) is one solution that addresses that need. After you install the module, you have the option to control metadata globally or by individual pages (the feature is tied to node creation). There are a number of options included with this module, as you can see in the configuration discussion later in this chapter.

 Note that the Meta Tags module requires the Token and Chaos Tools modules; you must download and install those modules first.

Page Title

The Page Title module (`http://drupal.org/project/page_title`) gives you control over the page title found inside the `<title>` tag inside the HTML head of your pages. The extension lets you create patterns that automatically construct the title string according to your criteria. The system even allows you to specify multiple patterns that will be applied depending upon context, allowing you to use different patterns in different situations.

Pathauto

The Pathauto module (`http://drupal.org/project/pathauto`) enhances your SEF URL efforts by automatically generating URL/path aliases for your nodes. The module allows you to set alias patterns and vary them according to node type (of course you can always override these manually on a case-by-case basis). See the discussion later in this chapter on configuration.

The Pathauto module depends upon the Path and Token modules. Both of the pre-requisites must be installed and enabled before you can use Pathauto.

Search 404

The Search 404 module (`http://drupal.org/project/search404`) gives you an alternative for handling 404 errors on your site. With this module installed, a site visitor who encounters a 404 error won't see the standard "404 Page Not Found" page, but instead, this module will perform a search on the keywords in the user's URL and show possible matches from your site.

SEO Checklist

The SEO Checklist module (`http://drupal.org/project/seo_checklist`) adds no additional functionality to your site, rather it provides a list of recommended Drupal SEO modules and helps expose their options in the administration system. If you are new to Drupal, or to SEO, the module helps you get off on the right foot. More experienced users may not find the module as useful.

SEO UI

SEO UI (`http://drupal.org/project/seo_ui`) is a utility module designed to consolidate the SEO options on the node editing screen and simplify the user interface for your content managers. The module offers no additional functionality; it is simply designed to make things easier for the content managers. Once installed, you can configure the module to gather the interfaces from the various SEO modules you have already installed and then group them into a single tab at the bottom of the node editing page, as seen in the following screenshot. The module supports integration of any of the following SEO modules:

- Meta Tags
- Path
- Pathauto

- Redirect

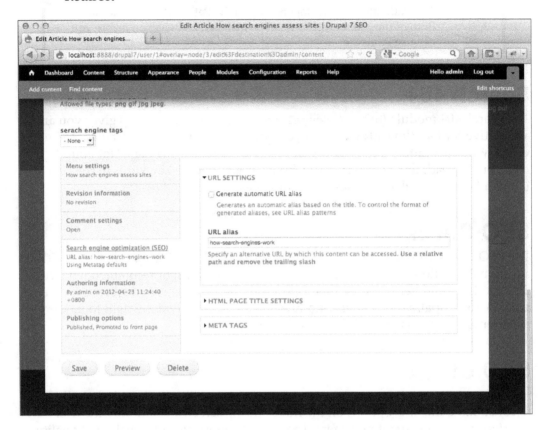

SEO Watcher

SEO Watcher (`http://drupal.org/project/seowatcher`) is a different type of extension; its function is research and reporting. The module allows you to search specified keywords with major search engines and then check the rank of your site and your competitors for those words. You can specify up to 10 keywords and five competitor sites. The checks can be performed automatically with the reports e-mailed to the addresses you specify.

SexyBookmarks

SexyBookmarks (`http://drupal.org/project/sexybookmarks`) includes integration for more than sixty of the most popular social bookmarking and networking sites, including Facebook, Twitter, Digg, and Google+. The extension features a number of options for controlling the position and styling of the icons. You can also select the pages where you want the buttons to appear.

TagClouds

The TagClouds module (http://drupal.org/project/tagclouds) generates a configurable tag cloud, based upon the taxonomies of your site. There are several modules that offer this functionality; this is one of the simplest.

XML sitemap

XML sitemap (http://drupal.org/project/xmlsitemap) allows to automatically generate XML sitemaps for your site. Configuration options are extensive and let you select which items to include or exclude as well as the ability to set priority among them. The module also includes a sitemap submissions feature to make sure the search engines are notified whenever the contents of your site change. See the discussion later in this chapter on configuration.

 There are multiple submodules bundled with the XML sitemap module. Only enable the items you need.

Installing and configuring common SEO modules

In this section of the chapter, we're going to look at how you can achieve a number of key SEO optimization goals through the installation and configuration of a set of extensions. All of the extensions discussed are non-commercial and are available through the official Drupal site.

Taken together, the extensions listed previously will achieve the following enhancements to your site:

- Better SEF URL control
- Improved metadata management
- Improved title tag management
- Canonical URLs
- Creation of an XML sitemap
- Implementation of social bookmarking tools for your site visitors

If you implement these extensions, and also take full advantage of the clean URLs functionality in the Drupal core, you will be well on your way to having your site on solid SEO footing.

Enhancing SEF URLs

The clean URLs functionality delivered by the Path module in the Drupal core goes only part of the way towards providing you with solid search engine friendly URLs. The Pathauto module, discussed earlier in this chapter, provides the additional control that you will want to achieve optimal URL structures.

Pathauto gives you full control over your URL aliases, even allowing you to set up patterns that will be applied automatically. One of your first steps in setting up your Drupal site for SEO purposes is to install the Pathauto module.

To set up this module, follow the given steps:

1. Download and install the Pathauto module, discussed earlier.
2. Access the Module manager.
3. Find the module named **Pathauto**.
4. Click the checkbox in the **Enabled** column.
5. Click on the **Save configuration** button.
6. After the page reloads, scroll down to find the module again; this time, click on the **Configure** link next to the module name.
7. On the configuration screen, seen in the following screenshot, you can set the patterns you desire.
8. Set the patterns you want for the various types of content on your site.

 Click on the name of any of the items in the **Replacement Patterns** section, seen in the following screenshot, to view a list of additional tokens that are available for you to use in the construction of your URL alias patterns.

9. Click on the **Save Configuration** button.

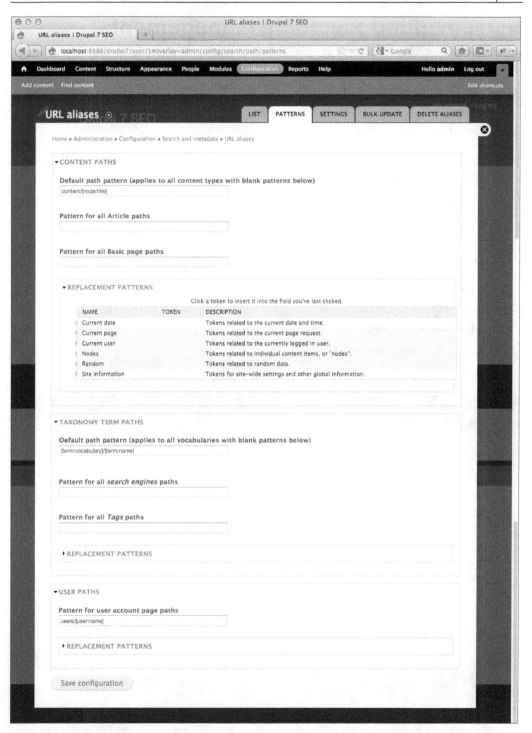

Implementing metadata management

As noted earlier, the default Drupal installation does not provide metadata management. Accordingly, you will want to install a module to add this functionality. The simplest option is the Meta Tags module. The extension gives you the ability to control your metadata fields either globally, or individually.

To set this module, follow the given steps:

1. Download and install the Meta Tags module, discussed earlier.

2. Access the Module Manager.

3. Find the module named **Meta tags**.

4. Click on the checkbox in the **Enabled** column.

5. Click on the **Save configuration** button.

6. After the page reloads, scroll down to find the module again; this time, click on the **Configure** link next to the module name.

7. On the configuration screen, as seen in the following screenshot, click on the link **Override**, next to the name of the category you wish to modify.

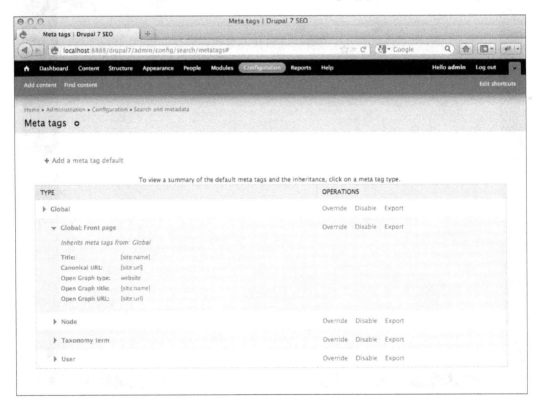

8. You will definitely want to set options for the choice **Global**, as these will provide the fall back metadata for the site—it will be used when nothing more specific is provided. You will also want to override the settings for **Global: Front page**, as this allows you to edit your home page metadata, arguably the most critical for your site.

9. Override the other sections as you see fit.

10. Click on the **Save** button.

At the conclusion of this configuration process, you will have data and patterns in place to populate your site's metadata fields. However, for optimal results, you will want to vary the metadata for each of your content items. Metadata should reflect accurately the content of individual pages, hence you should not use exactly the same metadata for all your content items. With the Meta Tags module installed, you will also be able to edit the metadata for each content item, either at the time you create the item or when you edit it.

> Exactly which fields you want to use is largely up to you. The most critical are the description and keywords fields, but you may want to consider the other options as well. The **Open Graph** section will help make sure that links to your pages display properly when people publish links to your site on various social media platforms, such as Facebook. The **Advanced** tab, gives you control over the indexing of the page contents. Be careful here not to block the spiders from indexing your pages! In the next chapter we look at metadata field options in more detail.

Improving Title Tag management

Control over your page titles, via the `<title>` tag, is critical for your SEO efforts. Page titles are very influential on your rankings and also useful for your site visitors. The Page Title module provides you with the ability to create custom page titles for your content. The module enables you to set patterns that automate the creation of page titles, while still allowing you to customize the titles at the time the item is created or edited.

To implement this functionality, install and configure the module, as per the following steps:

1. Download and install the Page Title module, discussed earlier.

2. Access the Module manager.

3. Find the module named **Page Title**.

4. Click on the checkbox in the **Enabled** column.

5. Click on the **Save configuration** button.

6. After the page reloads, scroll down to find the module again; this time, click on the **Configure** link next to the module name.

7. On the configuration screen, you can create patterns for your home page and for different types of internal pages. Note at the bottom of the page a list of all the available tokens you can use in creating the patterns for your page titles.

8. When you are finished, click on the **Save configuration** button.

Title Tag tips

Some tips for Title Tag are as follows:

- Use keyphrases in your page titles
- The title should reflect the page contents
- Start the title with the keyphrase
- Don't over-optimize the title by trying to cram in too many keywords
- Keep page title length to no more than 70 characters

Though it's not required, if you have the Token module installed, you will have a wider range of options for automated Page Title creation.

Setting up Canonical URLs

Oftentimes, particularly in complex sites, there may be multiple ways to arrive at a single content item. For SEO purposes, you want to force all the URLs in the content item to use the same structure. This is not only a best practice issue but also a way to reduce confusion and the possibility that your site may contain duplicate content. The practice of standardizing the URL structure is known as creating canonical URLs.

The Global Redirect module provides canonicalization, as well as additional benefits. With the module installed, enabled, and configured, you can not only remove the threat of duplicate content, but also help enforce clean URLs, control access to content, remove trailing slashes, and more. To set up the module, follow the given steps:

1. Download and install the Global Redirect module, discussed earlier.

2. Access the Module manager.

3. Find the module named **Global Redirect**.

4. Click on the checkbox in the **Enabled** column.

5. Click on the **Save configuration** button.

6. After the page reloads, scroll down to find the module again; this time, click on the **Configure** link next to the module name.

7. On the configuration screen, as seen in the following screenshot, select the options you desire. Make sure you click on the option **Add Canonical Link**.

8. Click on the **Save Configuration** button.

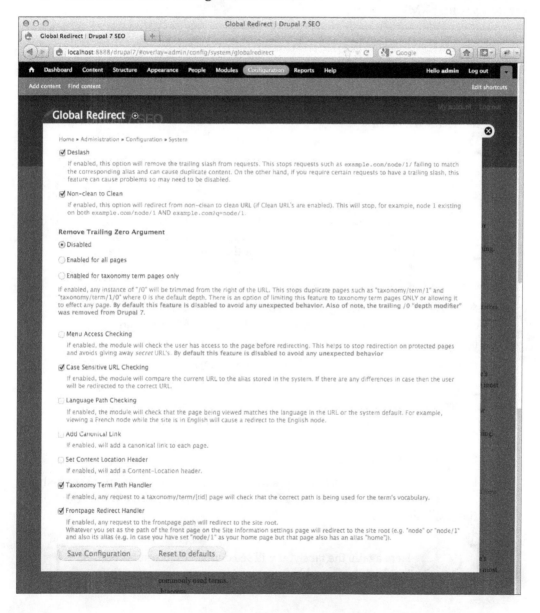

Setting up your XML sitemap

XML sitemaps are an essential element of your SEO strategy. All the major search engines implement the XML sitemaps standard and you will certainly want to follow it on your site. The XML Sitemap component, described earlier, gives you a simple way to implement this key functionality. Follow the given steps to get started and create your first XML sitemap:

1. Download and install the XML Sitemap module, discussed earlier.

2. Access the Module manager.

3. Find the module named **XML Sitemap**.

4. Click on the checkbox in the **Enabled** column for the primary module, named **XML sitemap**.

> There are a number of additional sub modules available here; select the ones you want to use. If you want the module to automatically submit the sitemaps for you, then enable the sub module named **XML sitemap engines**. Other sub modules add menu items, comments, users, and more to your sitemap. You may want some of these options, but it's unlikely you will have need for them all.

5. Click on the **Save configuration** button.

6. After the page reloads, scroll down to find the module again; this time, click on the **Configure** link next to the module **XML sitemap**.

7. When the XML sitemap configuration page loads, you will note at the top a set of tabs: **List, Custom Links, Settings**, and **Rebuild Links**.

> If you have selected the XML sitemap engines submodule, then you will also see a tab labeled **Search Engines**.

8. Click on the **Settings** tab.

9. Use the tabs at the bottom of the screen, as seen in the following screenshot, and set the **Priority** and **Change frequency** for the various items listed on the XML sitemap.

> Here again, the tabs you will see depend on the submodules that have been enabled.

10. When finished, click on the **Save configuration** button.

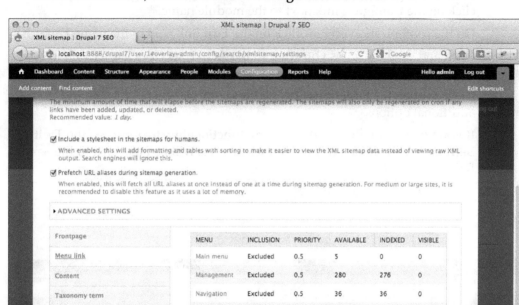

Providing social bookmarking

Mentions of your site on social networks and social bookmarking sites are important influencers in your SEO relevancy ranking. Use the SexyBookmarks module to add links to the most common services on your content pages and make it easy for site visitors to help spread the word about your site's contents.

To set up the extension, follow the given steps:

1. Download and install the SexyBookmarks module, discussed earlier.
2. Access the Module manager.
3. Find the module named **SexyBookmarks**.
4. Click on the checkbox in the **Enabled** column.
5. Click on the **Save configuration** button.

6. After the page reloads, scroll down to find the module again; this time, click on the **Configure** link next to the module name.

7. On the configuration screen, click on the **Edit** link next to the name **Default**.

8. Click and drag the icons you want to the **Active services** list, as seen in the following screenshot.

9. Click to open the **Functionality Settings** controls where you can find additional options.

10. If you want to use the Twitter posting functionality, toggle open the **Twitter Settings** section and configure the way tweets will be posted from the Sexy Bookmarks links.

11. Click on the **Save** button.

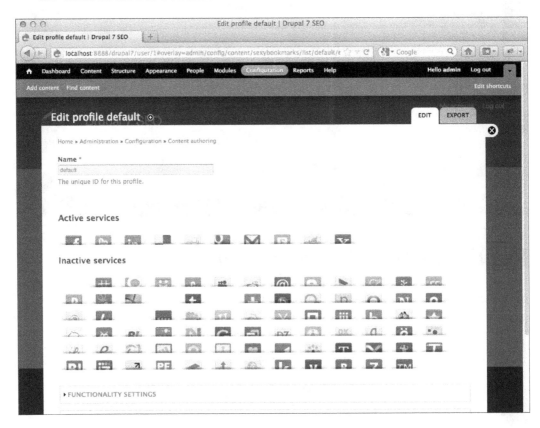

 Among the options available in the **Active services** are a "print this page" link and an "email to a friend" functionality.

Summary

In this chapter we've looked at how you can add modules to your site to enhance search engine optimization. We focused our attention on the modules available free of charge through the official Drupal site.

This chapter identified the top SEO extensions for Drupal 7.x and described what they can do for you. We then showed you how to install and configure a specific set of those modules to create a solid foundation for your SEO efforts.

In the next chapter we will discuss what you need to do to get ready to launch your site; that is, the hands-on SEO work you should do in the lead up to launching (or re-launching) a site.

4
Getting Ready for Launch

In previous chapters, we focused our discussion on the tools you need to get your site technically prepared for an SEO campaign. This chapter focuses on the strategy side of things. We look at the decisions you need to make to create an effective SEO strategy for your site, how to implement that strategy, and how to get your site ready for launch.

The first portion of the chapter is focused on high level planning, with an extensive discussion of approaches to keyword selection and a recommended process. Once you've decided on your keyphrases, you need to liaise with the content creators to assure that your search engine strategy is reflected in your content creation efforts and your metadata management. In the second part of the chapter we look at the role content creation plays in SEO. In the final portion of the chapter we look at some useful third-party tools that can assist you with getting your site into the search engines and thereafter assist with monitoring and tracking your efforts.

Determining your SEO strategy

Do not underestimate the importance of having a coherent SEO strategy. As we have stated several times in this book, SEO is a process. Like any process, you need to establish a set of parameters that guide the execution team and help assure that your efforts are coordinated and therefore most likely to advance your overall goals. There are many factors that affect a site's search engine optimization, hence, no part of the process exists in isolation and it is necessary to make sure all your efforts move in harmony.

Identifying keywords and phrases

For most companies, the initial steps in setting an SEO strategy focus on defining the product priorities and the target markets. As those issues are typically driven by the specific concerns of individual businesses, we're going to focus this discussion on the next step in the strategy process, that is, determining which keywords and phrases are most likely to deliver the type of traffic the site needs.

Start the keyword selection process by thinking big—don't restrict yourself by trying to formulate from the outset the most exact and narrow keyphrases, rather, come up with a large set of potentially relevant words and phrases that you can then whittle down to the optimal set. Look at the product or service, consider language variants, the terms of art, the related concepts. Make a list and add to it over time; this is one of those exercises that tends to benefit from a bit of time to think about things and process them. It's also a good idea to get other people involved to help offset subjective bias.

After you've assembled your preliminary list, it's best to take some time and do some research to make sure you haven't missed any candidate words or phrases. To accomplish this we'll use several techniques. One of the easiest ways to search for keyphrase ideas is to look at what is being done by your competitors. To do this, simply identify a set of competitors, visit their sites, and then view the source code to see what, if anything, is in their metadata. Add any new discoveries to your master list.

A second technique is to use the Google AdWords Keyword tool. The tool is free of charge and, despite the name, it's useful for a lot more than AdWords. Here's how to use it:

1. Direct your browser to `https://adwords.google.com/select/KeywordToolExternal`.

 Though you don't need to log in to Google to use the tool, you probably want to, as it unlocks additional functionality.

2. Open your list of potential keywords and copy the list.

3. Paste the list in the field marked **Word or phrase**, as seen in the following screenshot. Put each word or phrase on a separate line.

4. Modify the **Advanced Options and Filters** field to reflect the countries where your target markets reside and select the appropriate language and devices.

5. Complete the anti-spam CAPTCHA field. (You won't see this if you are logged in to Google.)

6. Click on the **Search** button.

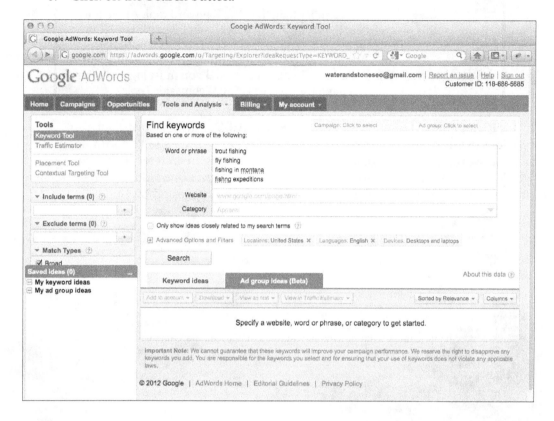

The tool will then present you with a (potentially) long list of words and phrases that are related to your ideas, along with data about how frequently they were used by people searching the Google search engine.

As an alternative to entering words or phrases as your starting point for keyword ideas, you can also point the tool to a particular web address. To use the website discovery tool, follow the given steps:

1. Type the address of a competitor or other relevant website into the **Website** field.

2. Select the **Advanced Options and Filters**, as discussed previously.

3. Complete the anti-spam CAPTCHA field, if it appears.

4. Click on the **Search** button.

Again, the tool presents you with a list of potential words and phrases, this time based on the content of a specific web page — a useful way to cross check your keyword ideas and discover new potential sources of traffic.

Bing now offers a similar tool, the Bing Keyword tool. At the time this was written, the tool was still in beta, but looks quite useful. You can access the tool at `http://www.bing.com/toolbox/keywords`. Note that to use the Keyword tool, you must first have a Bing Webmaster Tools account and you must log in. In the last part of this chapter we discuss Bing Webmaster Tools.

In addition to the list of words and phrases, the AdWords Keyword Tool also provides other useful information. The following screenshot shows a sample result set. The six words at the top, located under the heading **Search terms**, are the six words I entered into the **Word or phrase** field. The eight hundred (!) words and phrases under the heading **Keyword ideas**, are those suggested by Google.

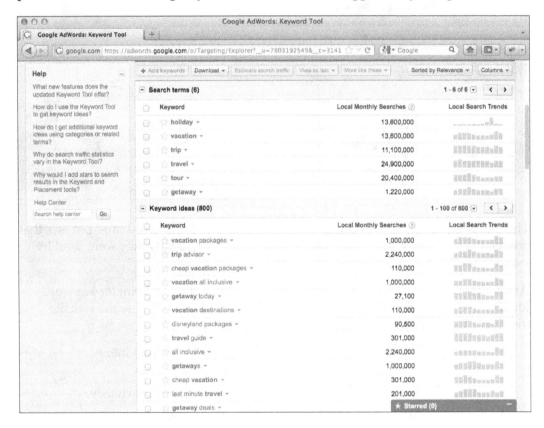

The two columns to the right of the keywords are important. The first, **Local Monthly Searches**, displays the number of times this keyword or phrase was entered into the Google search engine by a visitor; the number is a monthly average over the last 12 months.

"Local" in this context, reflects the target markets you selected in the **Advanced Options and Filters** section when you submitted your search in the Keyword tool.

Click the combo box labeled **Sorted by Relevance** to change the sort criteria for the list of keywords, allowing you to easily spot the most popular keywords. You can now identify with confidence the keywords that are associated with the most traffic.

 Using the **Columns** combo box, seen at the top right of the previous screenshot, you can select to view additional columns of data. One of the options allows you to display the average monthly traffic globally. This is a useful metric that allows you to compare global volume with the local volume.

The final column, **Local Search Trends**, contains 12 bars that display the relative search volume for the keyword in your target markets for each of the last 12 months; a useful way of identifying trending terms.

Targeting Trends

If you are aggressively marketing products or services, you will want to try to take advantages of transient trends in search interest. As timeliness is key, trend spotting for SEO purposes is best accomplished through research of real time and near real time services. Social media sites are often your best source of information about what's hot right now.

One of your best options for spotting trending topics is the Twitter Trends information provided to logged in users by Twitter. While the default shows the top trending global topics, you can also filter the list by country and in some cases, by specific cities. This information appears on your Twitter account home page.

Another option is the Google Hot Trends page, which gives you a daily breakdown of the most popular searches. While the tool is free, it is very limited in that it only provides insights into broad search patterns and does not allow for granular or geographic filtering of the results. Explore Hot Trends at http://www.google.com/trends/hottrends.

Another tool from Google is called Google Insights for Search (http://www.google.com/insights/search/). While this tool is not terribly convenient for discovering transient trends, it is useful for validating and quantifying trends. It also allows for filtering by date and location, which can be used to fine-tune your targeting.

Now that you have a set of keywords that have a known ability to deliver traffic, you need to select which ones to target for your efforts. You're not going to be able to target all the relevant, or even necessarily the most desirable, keyphrases. For most people, this comes down to a cost/benefit analysis. Be selective and pick a limited set that represents the best choices for your site.

If you are like most people, at this point you will want to get your keywords data out of the Google Keyword Tool and into a tool that allows you to manipulate the data more easily. Google makes this easy to do; simply click on the checkbox next to the words you want to keep, then click on the **Download** button and select the format for the file. You will then be able to open the keyword list and manipulate it in Excel, or your preferred spreadsheet program. If you don't see the **Download** option, log in to Google.

Note that the Google AdWords External Keyword Tool is only one tool for identifying potential keywords for your site. While the Google tool enjoys the benefit of being free of charge, if you are out to be more competitive and dig more deeply into keyphrase research, you will want to explore commercial offerings like SEMrush (http://www.semrush.com), Trellian KW Discovery tool (http://www.keyworddiscovery.com/), WordStream (http://www.wordstream.com/keywords), or Wordtracker (http://www.wordtracker.com/). Another useful free tool is Ubersuggest (http://ubersuggest.org/).

The decision as to which keyphrases are the best choice for any particular site is a subjective one. If you are concerned about fast results or responding to seasonal demand patterns, you will be looking at trending keyphrases and those with high volume. If you are looking at long-term brand building or product awareness, you may be selecting words that most accurately describe your products or services, regardless of whether those terms generate less traffic than other less specific keywords.

How many keywords?

How many keywords or phrases should you target? The answer is: it depends. Generally, a large site with significant content has more opportunities for traffic acquisition via keyword optimization. It's simple math: the more content (and the broader the content), the more potentially relevant keywords. A good rule of thumb is to not attempt to target more than two or three keyphrases for any single URL.

You can be certain that you are not the only person who has determined that a particular keyphrase is valuable. There will always be competition. While you can blindly pursue the highest volume keyphrases without consideration of the competition for those phrases, we cannot recommend that approach; it is a recipe for slow, or no, results. If you wish to target high traffic, high competition keywords, be prepared for a long fight for ranking (and thereafter an on-going struggle to maintain those rankings). The low-hanging fruit is in the long tail, that is, the keyphrases found near the narrow end of the search query frequency or competition distribution. Visually, the distribution of search terms typically follows the pattern seen next. **The Long Tail** consists of the queries to the far right of the curve.

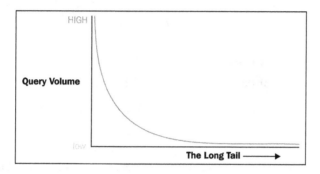

Chasing the long tail has several advantages, as follows:

- Competition tends to be lower, thereby increasing your chances of ranking well

- Conversion rates tend to be higher, typically because there is a correlation between the length (or specificity, if you prefer) of the keyphrase and its position on the tail, that is, the longer the keyphrase, the further it is towards the end of the tail

 The long tail is typically populated by longer, more specific keyphrases.

Reaping the rewards of a long tail is much easier than competing against large number of sites for broad keywords. While there are, literally, millions of sites competing for the phrase `caribbean villa`, there are significantly fewer chasing the phrase `2 bedroom villa for rent in Curacao`. Moreover, if someone is looking specifically to rent a two bedroom villa in Curacao, and you have one available on your site, then this is just the sort of visitor you want. In contrast, if someone is simply searching for `caribbean villa`, you have no idea what island is of interest, or even whether they want to rent or buy. In other words, they may not be the customers you are looking for.

Assessing keyword effectiveness

While keyphrase selection is more an art than a science, there are metrics you can apply to the process. One of the most useful is known as the keyword effectiveness index, or KEI. KEI, in its simplest form, is a comparison of the potential search volume for a term relative to the number of pages competing for that term.

There are multiple methodologies for determining KEI; which approach you prefer will typically depend on your personal SEO strategy. The most direct KEI formula looks like this:

KEI = V2/C

Where:

- V is the volume of search queries for the term
- C is the number of pages competing for the term

In other words, the square of the search query volume divided by the number of competing pages.

> Why do we use the square of the volume figure? This is done in order to take into account the popularity of the query. Without the multiplier, a term that averages only two queries a month, but has 100 competitors, would get the same KEI as a term that averages 200 queries a month and has 10,000 competitors. This is anomalous, as the term with 200 queries a month is clearly the more desirable. By introducing a multiplier into the equation, we reward more popular queries with a higher KEI.

Let's put the formula into practice: If you look at the Google Keyword Tool screenshot earlier in this chapter, you can see that the search term **last minute travel** generated an average of **201,000** queries per month over the last year; that's the first piece of data we need. Now, we need to find the number of pages competing. To do that, simply go to Google and run a search for **last minute travel**. At the top of the search results, Google tells you how many results were found, as seen in the following screenshot:

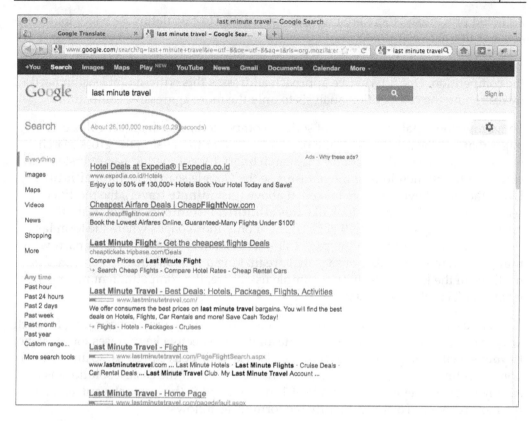

Now we have both of the numbers we need:

201,0002/26,100,000 = 1547.9

Accordingly, using this measure of keyword effectiveness, we can say that the phrase **last minute travel** has a KEI of 1547.9.

We could then run the rest of our candidate keyphrases through the same exercise and create an objective benchmark that could be used to compare the relative attractiveness of each of the various words and phrases.

In the example given, we looked to `Google.com` for data. Depending on your target markets, you may well want to check instead the country-specific versions of Google. Note that your choice of geographic filters in the Google Keyword Tool should be consistent with your selection of the appropriate Google search engine. In the example given, the Keyword Tool was set to produce results relevant to the United States, and the competition data was then taken from `Google.com`, as it is by far the most popular choice for web searches in the U.S. You should apply a similar logic if you are targeting non-U.S., or non-English-speaking markets. The important point here is be consistent: you want an apples to apples comparison.

As noted previously, there are multiple approaches to calculating KEI; let's look now at some alternative approaches.

The most common criticism of KEI is that it does not take into account the quality of the competition. One alternative approach addresses this criticism (at least in part) by restricting the competition analysis to only the more aggressive competitors.

To narrow your analysis to a list of serious competitors, search only for those pages that use the keyphrase in the page titles (rather than using the gross search results figure). To do this, modify the search query for competing pages. Instead of searching for all mentions of the phrase, use the Google search operator **allintitle**. Using the same keyphrase we looked at above (**last minute travel**), the modified search query to Google will look like this **allintitle: last minute travel**. With this operator in the query, you will get a count of only those pages where the term **last minute travel** is included in the page title—a reasonably effective way of narrowing things down to the number of sites that are making a serious effort to compete for traffic from the keyphrase. In the example used here, the competition number drops from over 26 million to 767,000.

Another useful variation on the KEI formula is to factor in a relevance rating for each keyphrase. To do this, you must first rate all the prospective keyphrases for relevance to your specific site (or page, or product). This is a subjective process, so any criteria you use is fine, as long as it is logically consistent. One of the easiest solutions is to simply rate each keyword on a scale of 1 to 3, where 1 is the least relevant, and 3 is the most relevant. To apply, modify the formula as follows:

$$KEI = (V2/C)R$$

Where:

- V is the volume of search queries for the term
- C is the number of pages competing for the term
- R is your relevance ranking

In other words, take the square of the search query volume, divide it by the number of competing pages, and then finally multiply the result by the relevance ranking.

Of course, you can always combine both of these variations, or you can create your own version of this popular formula. Regardless of which path you choose, using an objective metric to assess the possible keyphrases is a useful exercise. Not only does it allow you to impose a transparent methodology on your keyword selection process, but also it helps decision makers formulate an appropriate cost/benefit analysis for chasing particular keyphrases.

One final point—and it should go without saying—never forget that the suitability of content is always an issue. It does you no good to blindly select keywords based solely on search volume or KEI; to see success, the phrases must be relevant to the content on the URL you are targeting.

Tapping into the power of stemming and variants

The major search engines are, to varying degrees, capable of identifying similar and related words. You can use this to your advantage in both your keyphrase selection strategy and in your content creation. Two techniques are of primary use here: stemming and word variants.

Stemming is simply reducing a word to its root form. To take a simple example, the word "take" has multiple acceptable forms: take, taken, taking, and took. Other words have irregular plural forms, for example, "child" and "children." In these examples, "take" and "child" would be considered to be the root forms.

Most search engines will recognize the various grammatical forms and derivations of a root and return them as relevant results when a user searches for the root word (though the variants will typically rank lower for relevance than search results containing the exact root).

Variants, in this context, refers to the use of synonyms, alternative spellings, and common misspellings. As with stemming, you should always investigate the options presented by variants in your assessment of the optimal keyphrases. Synonym usage, in particular, can often provide very fertile ground. Differences in British and American English are also an area that should be investigated, particularly where your target markets use mixed (some spell it one way, others, another) spellings. Misspellings can also provide some pleasant surprises, opening up low competition avenues to search engine traffic.

In terms of keyword strategy, there's an opportunity here: your search for the optimal keywords should also look at the word roots that are relevant to your site and compare the traffic for the roots against the other forms to find the optimal mix. Based on the results, you can decide whether to target the root, or a specific derivation.

In terms of content creation, an awareness of this issue gives webmasters more latitude when writing content, empowering the use of alternative forms that are closely related. By varying your word choice in your content, you can avoid boring repetitions that alienate readers and keyword stuffing that alienates search engines.

Does capitalization matter?

Yes, it does, in certain narrow instances. Traditionally in search, if a user entered a query in lower case, the engine returned all results, both upper and lower case. If the user entered upper case (capitalized text), the search engine returned upper case results. The logic for this was simple: Words entirely in capitals are most likely acronyms, with distinct or specialized meanings. Words in title case (that is, only the first letter capitalized), most likely refer to proper names, including places or brands.

While Google and other major search engines exhibit much more flexibility and no longer implement the rule strictly (at least in basic search), your use of capitalization should reflect accurately the content. If you are dealing with a person, place, or brand, use title case. If you are dealing with an acronym, use all caps. For everything else, use lower case. Moreover, if you are targeting niche search engines or legacy information retrieval systems, you may still find these search conventions in force.

Content strategies for enhancing search engine ranking

The old cliché "content is king" managed to become both old and a cliché by benefitting from an additional attribute: accuracy. The search engines themselves, despite being notoriously reluctant to share insights into their priorities, have consistently made it clear that they consider the content of your site the most influential attribute in keyphrase relevance and ranking. It's no joke: when it comes to SEO, content is the undisputed king.

The issue of the importance of content has multiple facets; don't make the mistake of thinking that is enough to simply have large amounts of content. There are three aspects of content that greatly affect the amount of influence it has on a site's ranking: relevancy, recency, and quantity.

Relevancy is the top priority. If you want to rank well for the phrase `vintage mustang parts`, then your page had better contain information about vintage mustang parts. A single mention of the keyphrase on the page isn't going to do the job either; the content needs to discuss the topic in some detail to get the maximum benefit from the presence of related words and phrases—something the search engines look to as context clues that help them dial in the relevance for a page (also sometimes referred to as "block analysis," whereby search engines determine meaning not from simple phrases or sentences, but from entire blocks of text).

The concept of keyword density is worth mentioning here. The phrase refers to the percentage of times that a keyword or phrase appears on a page. The theory is that with too many keywords on the page you will risk being penalized for keyword stuffing; too few and your relevance ranking suffers. Calculating a page's keyword density is simple: count the number of times a particular word or phrase is mentioned on the page, then divide by the total number of words on the page. This topic is not without controversy, however. Some SEO experts consider optimum density to be in the range of .002 to .004. Others say it just doesn't matter, and that keyword density is a stale concept. From our perspective, obsessing on keyword density is probably not the best use of your time. Today's search engines seem to attach less importance to frequency and rather more weight to the occurrence of terms in the top portion of the content item, in the headings, and of course, in the page title and URL. Work on creating natural, readable text and be concerned more with the prominence and position of the keywords on the page, than with the density. There is one thing everyone agrees on, however: don't keyword stuff!

Another key factor is the recency and frequency of change of your content. While this is more of concern for the webmaster post-launch, it's relevant to the discussion here. It is widely believed that the search engines not only assess how recently the page was updated, but also the frequency with which the content on the site changes and how that update rate changes from period to period. Accordingly, an on-going challenge for your webmaster is the creation of new pages and the updating of stale ones. As new pages are created, make sure you add internal links to and/or from older pages, both to improve internal link density and to encourage people to explore your site further.

The concept is pretty straightforward, but to put it into an easy-to-use list, here are the important points:

- Create new content. Adding new pages at a higher rate than your competitors gives an advantage.
- Update old content regularly.
- The larger the extent of an update to a page, the better.
- The frequency of change is a factor; more frequent changes are better.
- Changes to content above the fold are more important than changes in less important areas of the page.

The final factor to discuss here is quantity, and this is by far the simplest point. In short: More is better! All things being equal, a site with more relevant content enjoys an advantage over its competitors. Note this important caveat: when we talk here about content, we mean quality, original content. Merely reproducing articles that appear elsewhere on the Web is not a valid content strategy for boosting your site's rankings. Similarly, creating tons of low quality or repetitive content won't help you either, instead, it's more likely to hurt you.

The importance of a concerted effort

While you should be concerned about the quality of your content, do not lose sight of the fact that a highly effective site is the result of a number of factors working in concert. Not only do you need to be concerned about the technical issues discussed in the previous chapters, but you also need to make sure that all your efforts are made in light of your overall strategy and are consistent in their emphasis of your target concepts.

When it comes to creating content, don't neglect the other elements on that page, as some of those are significant influencers on perceptions of relevance. These are as follows:

- The article's title is key. It should employ the keyphrase and it should be formatted with an appropriate H tag (probably H2). H tags are interpreted by the search engines as indicators of importance, hence they should be used to provide signals as to what is most important on the page and how those points are related to each other.

- Similarly, any subheading in the article should try to employ the keyphrase or variants and should employ H tags (probably H3, H4, H5, and so on).

- The page's URL is also key and should reflect the keyphrase.

- Links pointing to the page (internal or inbound) should employ relevant link text and should use the `title` attribute.

- Images on the page should have captions and `alt` attribute text that reinforce the keyphrase or related concept. (The name of the image file itself is also useful, particularly for ranking in Google Image Search.)

- The metadata for the page should be consistent with the page content and reinforce key concepts, picking up variants and stems.

- You should post links back to the content on social media sites when you publish the content.

- Make sure you update your XML sitemap to include new content items.

[In the previous discussion, what happened to the H1 tag? Simple. Best practice is to use that tag for your site name and/or tagline.]

Managing metadata

Metadata is used to describe the contents of a page. In the past, metadata played a key role in helping search engines understand the nature and content of pages, but today it plays a less critical role. Despite its decreasing importance, metadata should never be ignored; it is the one technical feature of pages that is purely intended to help understand and categorize the page content and therefore should always be used to further your SEO goals.

Metadata is added to pages through the use of meta tags, which appear in the head of the HTML document. While the W3C metadata standards provide for a wide range of possible meta tags, you will need to install an extension to fully control the metadata of your Drupal site. Different modules give you different options, but the key tags you will want to implement on your site are shown in the following table:

Drupal label	Meta tag	Notes	Importance
Description	`meta name="description"`	Should describe the content of the page. Note that this tag is important as some search engines display this as the description of the link when it appears on the SERP. That also means you should make sure it is grammatical and uses proper punctuation.	High
Keywords	`meta name="keywords"`	List the keywords and phrases you are targeting for the page.	Medium

Drupal label	Meta tag	Notes	Importance
Robots	`meta name="robots"`	A substitute for the `robots.txt` file in terms of providing the search engines with instructions about what to index on your site. Your choices here are limited to: • Index, Follow • No index, Follow • Index, No follow • No index, No follow	Medium
Author	`meta name="author"`	Intended to contain the author of the HTML page and provide contact information.	Low

How long is too long?

While there aren't any clear maximum lengths for the data strings you put into your meta tags, there are some recommended lengths to keep in mind as follows:

- Title: 60 - 70 characters (Google and Bing display 69 characters in the SERP)
- Description: 150 - 160 characters (Google displays 156 characters in the SERP; Bing, 150)
- Keywords: 256 characters

Metadata values can be set globally or by specific page. In terms of SEO strategy, you should always strive to provide specific metadata for individual pages. Simply using the global metadata throughout the site is not optimal and causes you to miss opportunities. In contrast, when you tailor the metadata to the contents of each specific page, you stay true to the intended purpose of metadata and provide a broader range of related concepts that can strengthen your overall SEO strategy. Moreover, use of distinct values in the description fields means that when more than one of your pages shows up in the SERP, each page will have an appropriate description to help guide the users to the page that best fits their needs.

When you create, or edit, a content item, you will have the opportunity to specify metadata for that particular page. If you input data into the article metadata, it will override the global metadata for the site, at least for that particular page.

Setting up third-party services that can assist with SEO

Once your site is built and populated with content, but prior to launching for the general public, you will want to take some preliminary steps to get the site ready for the search engines. In this section of the chapter we highlight three helpful third-party tools you should put in place for launch:

- Google Analytics
- Google Webmaster Tools
- Bing Webmaster Tools

All three tools require you to have accounts on the various services (that is, Google and Bing). In this text, we'll assume you have already registered for accounts on Google and Bing and will be using those accounts to get things set up for your site.

If you are setting up a site that you intend hand off to a client, you will probably want to create a unique account for them, or use one of the client's existing accounts. Transferring ownership of accounts is problematic and best avoided.

Getting started with Google Analytics

Google Analytics is a website traffic tracking program. The tool is free of charge, loaded with features, and an excellent choice for most website owners. If you are not familiar with the service, you should take some time to explore the tutorials Google offers, as fluency with the tool can be of great benefit to your SEO efforts.

With Google Analytics on your site, you can track site visitor activity and discover where they came from, how long they spent on the site, and what they looked at on your site. The system also tracks inbound search traffic and provides you with invaluable feedback on which keywords are generating traffic for your site in which markets.

You can learn more at http://www.google.com/analytics/ where you can create a free account and explore the help resources provided by Google.

Implementing the service takes three steps:

1. Create a Google Analytics account for the domain.
2. Copy the tracking code provided by Google Analytics and add it to the pages of the site.
3. Verify the site.

> If you are working on rebuilding a site that already has Google Analytics in place, we advise against creating new Google Analytics account for the rebuild. The better option is generally to use the existing site's Analytics code, which thereby preserves the site's traffic history and allows you to benchmark against historical data after you launch the new site.

In Drupal there are several modules that allow you to avoid having to copy and paste code – you only need to add the Google I.D. to the module and it will handle getting the code into the right place on each of the pages. If you are not using one of the extensions that includes Google Analytics management, you will need to edit the files of your Drupal theme to add the code in the right place on the page. While it's hard to go wrong here, you should note the placement of the code: it belongs just before the closing `</head>` tag. If there are other scripts in the `<head>` section of your page, put them before the Google Analytics tracking code.

Once the code is inserted into your theme, check it by viewing the site in your browser and then viewing the page source. If you don't see the Google Analytics tracking code, go back and check your work and try again.

> Note that verifying the site can only be done if the site is online.

Working with Google Webmaster Tools

Google Webmaster Tools is a free service provided by Google to help site owners gain insights into their web pages' visibility on Google. The service provides information about when and how deeply the site was spidered and whether there were any errors found. From a pure SEO perspective, the service is also quite useful as it allows you to identify search query traffic and maintain a count of inbound links. Additionally, it provides a place for you to register your XML sitemap and monitor whether the sitemap is functioning properly.

Visit Google Webmaster Tools at https://www.google.com/webmasters/tools.

To get started with Google Webmaster Tools, you need to create an account and then verify ownership of the site. The system provides you with alternative ways to verify the site, but for most people the easiest will be to download the HTML file Google provides and then move it up to the root of the domain you are registering.

Once you have verified the site, you should take two further steps. First, let's connect our Google Analytics account and let the Webmaster Tools service share information with the Analytics service. Once you link the accounts, you'll be able to see Webmaster Tools data in your Google Analytics reports and you'll also be able to access Analytics report data directly from relevant pages inside Google Webmaster Tools.

To link the accounts, follow the given steps:

1. Log in to Google Webmaster Tools.
2. On the Webmaster Tools home page click on the **Manage Site** link (next to the name of the site you want to link) and select the option **Google Analytics property**.
3. On the page that loads, select the radio button next to the Analytics property you want to associate with the site.
4. Click on the **Save** button.

The next step to take after you have verified your account is to notify Google about the existence of your XML sitemap. To add your sitemap, follow the given steps:

1. Log in to Google Webmaster.
2. On the Webmaster Tools home page, click on the name of your site to open the site management page.
3. Select the option **Sitemaps**, under **Site configuration**.
4. On the page that loads, click on the **Add/Test Sitemap** button on the top right of the page.
5. In the pop-up that appears, enter the URL of your XML sitemap.
6. Click on the **Submit Sitemap** button.

That's all there is to it. Google will put the URL for your sitemap in the queue to be spidered and once it is spidered, the results will be viewable inside the Google Webmaster Tools system; if there were errors, they will also be shown.

 You will want to check back in a day or so to make sure your site map has been indexed properly, and if not, troubleshoot it.

In addition to its ability to help you track keyword traffic and inbound links, Google Webmaster Tools provides a set of useful diagnostic tools to help you keep your site fine-tuned. You will want to check into your account periodically to check for error reports, and to look at how your site is being spidered. It's a good idea to monitor the depth of the spidering and to make sure that all your pages are being indexed. The system contains additional tips to help you with issues like your robots.txt file, possible malware infestations, and canonical URL settings.

 One of the more interesting tools is the option to view your site as Google sees it. This allows you to check your site's code by looking at it in the same fashion that is seen by Google's indexing spider, the Googlebot. It's a simple way to make sure your most critical information is clearly visible to the spider and not buried under tons of irrelevant code, scripts, and other noise. To use this tool, select the option **View site as Googlebot**.

Working with Bing Webmaster Tools

Bing Webmaster Tools is essentially, a parallel service to Google Webmaster Tools. The service is provided free of charge by Bing and allows you to perform the same basic tasks you can find on Google Webmaster Tools. Indeed, there are more similarities between the services than differences; the key difference being that Bing Webmaster Tools provides data for both Bing and Yahoo!.

 Visit Bing Webmaster Tools at http://www.bing.com/toolbox/ webmaster/.

To set up Bing Webmaster Tools for your site, simply create an account for the domain and then verify your ownership of the site. The system provides several alternatives for verifying your ownership of the domain; the easiest is probably to upload the XML file that Bing provides during the setup process.

After your site is verified, it's time to add your XML sitemap. Follow the given steps:

1. Log in to Bing Webmaster Tools.

2. Click on the name of your site.

3. On the page that loads, click on the **Crawl** tab at the top of the page.

4. On the **Crawl Summary** page, click on the **Sitemaps (XML, Atom, RSS)** link, either at the top, under the tabs or in the left hand navigation column.

5. On the **Sitemaps** page, click on the **Add Feed** button.

6. Type the URL of your XML sitemap in the pop-up that appears.

7. Click on the **Submit** button.

Your XML sitemap is now queued to be crawled by the Bing spider; check back in a day or so to verify that it was successful and free from errors.

Summary

This chapter was the first to look at the soft factors—the strategy and planning side of SEO management. The key points here being that it is necessary to engage in planning to create a relevant and practical SEO strategy before you start your work, and to then implement that strategy in a consistent and structured fashion.

In this chapter we looked at techniques for selecting keywords and phrases, with an emphasis on using the Keyword Effectiveness Index (KEI). Once you have a solid strategy and a set of keywords, it's time to get to work. Content creation plays a critical role in SEO. We discussed the three factors that content managers should keep in mind: relevance, recency, and quantity. We also looked at how to create the metadata for your site's pages, in line with your SEO strategy.

Prior to launch, you should also put in place several tools that will help you monitor and maintain your site. We looked at what they do and how to get started with each of them. The three systems serve varying purposes. Google Analytics, is a powerful web traffic reporting tool that lets you monitor your site traffic and inbound keyphrase performance. Google Webmaster and Bing Webmaster provide a set of useful tools focused on assessing how the site is being indexed by the search engines and provide you with tools to monitor indexing and keep your XML sitemaps up to date.

At the end of this chapter, you should have a site that is ready for launch. In previous chapters we covered the technical foundations. In this chapter we talked about strategy and implementation. In the final chapter in this book, we will look at on-going maintenance and enhancement of your SEO efforts.

5
Managing SEO on a Live Site

As we discussed in *Chapter 1, An Introduction to Search Engine Optimization*, SEO is not something you can do once and then forget about. This chapter looks at the steps you should take to help enhance and maintain your ranking once the site has gone live as well as how to track and assess the success of your efforts.

Topics covered in this chapter include link building, social media optimization, and how to track and measure your SEO performance over time.

Link building

Link building should be part of your on-going efforts to generate traffic and improve your site's organic search ranking. Looking at link building in the context of SEO, your best bet for success lies in emphasizing growth in the number of quality links that point to your site. In short, the more high quality links you have pointing to your site, the better. The search engines' view on this point is simple: If your content is authoritative and valuable other people will link to it. If the people linking to your content are also viewed as being authoritative, then the search engines consider the value of their links to be greater than links from a low authority website.

While links have traditionally been important influencers on relevancy ranking, it's important to understand that not all links are equal, at least not in the eyes of the search engines. Recent changes in the Google algorithm have been aimed at rooting out artificial link building strategies and minimizing their ability to impact rank. From a best practices perspective, link building (or "link marketing" if you prefer) should not be viewed primarily as an exercise in manipulating rank, but rather as a means of increasing your site's influence and reach. Don't obsess on building the greatest number of links, rather, focus on building strategic links and exposing your high quality content to the widest range of people.

Watch out for nofollow!

nofollow is a value available to the link relation attribute of the HTML link or a elements. At the code level, the attribute looks like <a href="http://hyperlink.com" rel="nofollow">Link text</a>. When the nofollow value is specified in the rel attribute, search engines will not follow and index the link. In the event that nofollow is not specified, the search engine spiders will follow the link (assuming that the spiders have not been blocked from indexing in some other fashion).

In the context of link building, this is a crucial issue. Adding your link to a site that includes nofollow on links means that you gain no SEO benefit from the existence of the link. Before you add your link to a site, it is essential that you examine the site's source code to make sure that the outbound links are not using nofollow.

Links fall into three broad categories as follows:

- **Organic links**: These are links to your site that are voluntarily given by others. Organic links are normally a by-product of excellent content that people want to share.

- **Solicited links**: Links obtained by reaching out to another site and requesting a link. This would include links you purchase, reciprocal links, and other similar schemes.

- **Self-created links**: Links that you create by posting content on other sites. This category includes article submissions, press releases, forum posts, comments, and proactive social sharing.

Of the three, the latter are the easiest to obtain, as the act of link creation is completely within your control. The first two categories require effort over time and are really outside your control; whether you get the link is not up to you (unless, of course, you're buying the link). In the following sections, we look at how to identify potential link partners and how to structure a link building campaign.

Never lose site of the fact that ranking well on the search engines is merely a means to an end. For most site owners, the ultimate goal of engaging in an SEO campaign is the creation of relevant referral traffic, be it from search engines or from other sites. Links can be instrumental in driving qualified traffic and should be viewed primarily from this perspective.

Identifying quality link partners

The process of finding quality link partners begins with a search for relevant sites. The goal is to identify sites that will return the highest value in exchange for the amount of effort you have to invest to obtain the link. Once you have identified candidates, you must look at the value those links will generate and rank them as priorities for your efforts.

How do you find potential link partners? There are multiple techniques you can apply, but often the easiest is to first look at your competitors and identify the sites that have given them inbound links; the rationale being that if another site was interested in your competitors, they might very well be interested in you.

While there are tools that will help you spot inbound links to competitor sites, you can accomplish a lot on your own by simply going to Google and running a search on the competitor's domain name using the query parameter `link:`.

> To find all the pages linking to the site `packtpub.com`, for example, you would enter the query `link:packtpub.com` into the Google search field.

Once you have a list of all your competitors' inbound links, you can set out to contact them and request links to your content. Following the path laid down by your competitors is, however, the low-hanging fruit. You will most certainly want to do more.

If you don't have the time to manually search for your competitors' link partners, or you need to search a large number of domains, try using Open Site Explorer (`http://opensiteexplorer.org`). Simply enter the URL of your competitor's site and the system will return a list of all links related to that site. Filter the list to show only external links, then export the data as a `.csv` file. Once you import the `.csv` file into your favorite spreadsheet program, you have a list of your competitor's links, ready for you to contact.

> Note that you while you can use Open Site Explorer free of charge, you do have to be a subscriber to use the `.csv` download feature. Registration also unlocks more features.

If you want to go one step further, take the `.csv` file from Open Site Explorer and import it to LinkDetective (`http://www.linkdetective.com`). LinkDetective is a free service that leverages the data from Open Site Explorer. Using the tool, you can obtain in depth information about your competitors' links and which are the most attractive for you to target.

Following the paths trodden by your competitors is only one way to discover potential link partners. Google and Bing are two of your most valuable tools, allowing you to track down relevant sites by using a variety of search techniques. Running a simple search on your keywords is one way to find relevant sites with high ranking, but you may want to consider using several of Google's search parameters to refine your hunt. The parameters are as follows:

- Use **allintitle: keyword(s)** to find pages where your keywords appear in the page title

- Use **allinurl: keyword(s)** to restrict the search results to only those pages where the keywords are part of the URL

- Use **allinanchor: keyword(s)** to find links where the keywords appear in the anchor text for links

- Use **allintext: keyword(s)** to find pages that have the highest relevance for your keywords in the content of the page

Similar tools for some of these options exist on Bing and on other major search engines.

The process of discovering link partners requires creative thinking and research ability. Although using search parameters (like those outlined previously) is a good starting point, you will want to dive much deeper to find the best opportunities. BuzzStream provides a free Link Building Query Generator that can save you quite a bit of time. Simply enter information about your brand, your competitors, and your market, and the tool will generate a number of potentially useful queries for both Google and Bing. The tool is a great way to kick start your link prospecting. To try out the tool, visit http://tools.buzzstream.com/link-building-query-generator.

Once you have your list of potential link prospects, the next step is to assess which can deliver the most value to you. Not all links are of equal importance. As stated earlier, your emphasis should be on building quality links to your site, and quality links come from high value, authoritative sites. There are several useful metrics that can help you identify the most attractive link prospects. Among the best and most widely-used metrics are:

- Alexa Rank (http://alexa.com)

- MozRank (http://opensiteexplorer.org)

- MozTrust (http://opensiteexplorer.org)

- Google PageRank: Use the Google Toolbar (for Internet Explorer only, unfortunately)

It should go without saying, but to be an effective link partner (for SEO relevancy purposes) the site should be relevant and authoritative for the content on your site. If your site is about colonial furniture, for example, getting links from a site about fly-fishing won't be much help to you; even if the fly fishing site is highly rated, it is not authoritative on the subject of furniture.

Managing a link marketing campaign

Link building is undoubtedly the most tedious and frustrating part of any SEO campaign. Though automation programs exist, they are of extremely little use in obtaining quality links. Automated link submission systems are really intended to get you large numbers of links, not help you identify and approach authoritative sites. The systems typically target online directories and other sites that gather links and organize them topically. Few of those sites, however, provide you with quality inbound links. Many of those sites exist for no other purpose than for creating links and their indexes are filled with low quality, spammy websites. If you have a quality site, you don't want to be there and you should avoid them.

The most reliable approach building for high quality links is also the most traditional, that is, creating a relationship with a site's publisher. Direct e-mails to a site owner, or to authors on a site, are a great way to expand your network and introduce your content to influencers. Seek out other avenues of outreach as well. If the site offers a contact form, use that to introduce yourself to the site owner. Don't forget about the telephone—a phone call can sometimes produce results faster than any other means of contact.

Every site publisher is used to seeing their inbox fill up with generic form e-mails asking for links. It's a huge turnoff to receive form e-mails that show no attempt at personalization, no attempt to explain why creating a relationship is useful or appropriate, or even worse, horrid grammar and spelling. Publishers will—rightfully—throw those messages straight into the trash (or mark them as junk!). Effective outreach involves the personal touch and shows a clear effort to demonstrate value and relevance that would motivate a publisher to engage in a dialogue.

Your link building efforts will eat up a fair amount of time and will require follow up. Given that there are often delays in response times, it's important that you impose some structure on your efforts, else you tend to lose track of things and your effectiveness is diluted. While there are software tools to help with link discovery and with tracking your contacts and link requests, often the simplest tool is to create a spreadsheet and set up columns for the site name, URL, contact person, contact address, and contact history. Use the spreadsheet to log your efforts and create a schedule for follow up. It's a cheap, simple, and effective way to impose order on a link building campaign.

If you have the budget and the inclination to use a commercial tool for researching and managing your link building campaign, one of the more attractive options is Ontolo. The system is available on a monthly subscription basis and gives you access to their link discovery and campaign management dashboard. Ontolo includes a number of useful tools, including very good competitor analysis and tracking. To learn more, visit `http://ontolo.com`.

Another option, with more flexible pricing, is BuzzStream. Like Ontolo, BuzzStream helps you discover potential link partners and manage your campaigns. The system also keeps track of backlinks and helps you monitor the status of your links. To learn more, visit `http://buzzstream.com`.

Content creation also has an important role in link marketing. If you are able to inspire others to link to your site solely on the strength of your content, then you will be well ahead in the game. Moreover, one-way links given freely based on editorial content are effective ways to generate traffic. The content can take many forms, some of the best proven approaches for creating interesting content include:

- Top Ten lists
- "Best of" lists
- Humor
- Infographics
- Great photos
- Controversial articles
- "How to" tutorials

Creating content items designed to generate links is sometimes referred to as creating "link bait".

Creating your own links

There are literally tens of thousands of sites on the web that present opportunities for you to create your own links. These opportunities take a variety of forms such as:

- Directories
- Comments
- Forum posts
- Content aggregators
- "Submit your site" opportunities
- Press release distribution
- Article exchanges
- Video sharing sites
- Document sharing sites

Use these options to create a varied collection of inbound links and to raise the profile of your site. Don't waste these opportunities by posting spammy comments or blatant plugs, rather use them to establish your site as a relevant authority and source of useful information. Directly plugging your site, particularly in comments or forums, will earn nothing but deletion or a ban on your IP.

When embedding links back to your site, make an effort to write good anchor text. Your choice of anchor text should help reinforce your keyword strategy, but more importantly, it should be natural and should represent the actual content of the destination page. Google has given indications that it is sensitive to unnatural anchor text. Too many repetitions of the same phrase may, in fact, signal to Google that the links are artificial and therefore it will de-value them.

 When a search engine indexes a link, the anchor text in that link is viewed as an indicator of what the destination page is about.

Directories

One of the easiest ways to get links is to submit your site to some of the many directories on the web. Listing in major directories, such as the Yahoo! Directory (http://dir.yahoo.com) or Business.com (http://www.business.com), offers some benefit, but almost all of the quality directories with a broad content focus require a listing fee. If you have the budget, you may want to consider some of these broad (non-specialized) directories, as listing is assured upon payment of the fee.

The largest free directory, DMOZ (http://dmoz.org) is extremely slow to accept new sites and is largely an exercise in frustration.

Some of the best directories out there are, however, niche directories. These topical directories focus on a specific topic and are often viewed as relevant authority in their field. If your site is similar in topic, niche directories can provide worthwhile inbound links. Moreover, from a traffic generation point of view, topical directories can be good sources of quality traffic, regardless of whether they are significantly persuasive to your site's search engine ranking.

Though not technically directories, don't overlook sites that provide for their visitors' lists of relevant resources. These "mini-directories" are typically topical and often worth the effort of seeking out for their link value.

Identifying quality directories

Despite the proliferation of low-quality web directories, there are a few winners out there. How do you identify a quality directory?

Page ranking indicators are useful, but don't just look at the home page. You should always look at the rank of the page where your link will appear. Often you will find that while the directory's home page has a solid ranking, the page where your link will appear has a much less desirable rank; if that's the case, think carefully about how much value this will deliver to you.

Finally, trust your instincts. How does the directory look to you? Is the appearance high quality? Is it current? Is it filled with spammy websites? Would you trust it for a site recommendation? If it looks dodgy and feels dodgy, it probably is dodgy – avoid it.

Press releases

Press releases, video sharing, and file sharing deserve special mention. While the creation of the content to feed these services is time consuming, the rewards can be significant. There are a number of useful free press release distribution services, including:

- Free Press Release (http://free-press-release.com)
- i-Newswire (http://i-newswire.com)
- PRinside (http://pr-inside.com)
- PRLog (http://prlog.org)

Posting your press release on those sites will get the releases indexed quickly. Moreover, some offer premium plans that add social bookmarking and other advanced indexing features. In addition to the free services, there are several very good commercial services worth considering, including PRWeb (`http://www.prweb.com`), PRLeap (`http://www.prleap.com`), and WebWire (`http://www.webwire.com`). These services offer expedited listings, expanded distribution and options for adding supplementary media.

 When you set up your press release, make sure you use the contact information section to add links and descriptive text.

Video and file sharing

Video and file sharing sites can be excellent sources of traffic. While YouTube is the big brand in the video world, don't forget about the large number of additional sites for distributing your video content, in particular:

- Dailymotion (`http://dailymotion.com`)
- Metacafe (`http://metacafe.com`)
- Photobucket (`http://photobucket.com`)
- Veoh (`http://veoh.com`)
- Vimeo (`http://vimeo.com`)

Photo sharing offers another option to create traffic and, in some cases, links. Use the photos as a resource for your other efforts, as well, linking to the image in social bookmarking sites, social media, and blog posts. The description field for the image also gives you a place to add descriptive copy.

The following are some of the leading photo sharing sites:

- Flickr (`http://flickr.com`)
- Photobucket (`http://photobucket.com`)
- Picasa (`http://picasa.google.com`)
- Pinterest (`http://pinterest.com`)
- SmugMug (`http://smugmug.com`)

Like video sharing, document and presentation sharing can be labor intensive but can also be worth the effort. A great document or slideshow presentation can drive good traffic to your site.

[While you can upload files in a variety of formats, typically PDFs work best as they not only maintain their formatting well, but can hold active links, too.]

Some of the more popular document sharing sites include:

- Docstoc (`http://www.docstoc.com`)
- Issuu (`http://issuu.com`)
- Scribd (`http://scribd.com`)
- Slideshare (`http://slideshare.net`)

 [When you set up your bio on your file sharing sites, use the contact information section to add links and descriptive text.]

Social media optimization

Social media has grown to take a significant role in search marketing. Your site should be optimized for social media, making it easy for your site visitors to save, share, and comment on your content. Take advantage of the trend in social interaction:

- Make it easy to recommend or share your content on the most popular social networks
- Facilitate bookmarking and tagging
- Provide comment functionality, monitor, and interact
- For rich media, make it easy for others to share it with their friends and site visitors
- Offer subscription functionality, whether by e-mail, or RSS, or both

 [Drupal provides several extensions that make it easy for you to add share buttons on your content items. Implement those extensions and make sure the buttons are available on all your content items. See *Chapter 3, Useful Extensions to Enhance SEO*, for a list of suggestions.]

As the webmaster of a site, you should make social media part of your content management strategy. One of your goals in content creation is to motivate users to share and recommend the content, thereby extending your site's reach into the users' social circles. Moreover, be proactive: After you add a content item to your site, publicize it via social media channels with links and tags that are consistent with the site's SEO goals.

The use of social channels to drive traffic, combined with the presence of social sharing tools on the site itself, creates a push and pull dynamic that will help you leverage your site's contents to the largest number of visitors, creating both inbound links and traffic. Done properly, and backed by compelling content, social media optimization can drive big traffic gains very quickly.

Social media optimization (**SMO**) is not just about creating new links to your content. It is about traffic generation, PR, reputation management, and crisis communications; all of these factors need to be considered in the creation of your SMO strategy.

As a content publisher, you should consider proactive sharing of your content on some, or all of the following:

- Delicious (http://delicious.com)
- Digg (http://digg.com)
- Facebook (http://facebook.com)
- Fark (http://fark.com)
- Google + (http://plus.google.com)
- Hackernews (http://hackerne.ws)
- LinkedIn (http://linkedin.com)
- Newsvine (http://newsvine.com)
- Pinterest (http://pinterest.com)
- Twitter (http://twitter.com)
- Reddit (http://reddit.com)
- StumbleUpon (http://stumbleupon.com)

Creating profiles

The past few years have brought a massive proliferation in the number of social media publishing channels. While old standards, such as Technorati and Digg, are still vital, there is a huge number of new channels. How do you decide which of those channels are important to you? How many is too many? The right answer is going to depend on your goals and the time you have to invest in these channels. It's a trade-off, a cost/benefit decision.

At the very least, you should try to maintain profiles (and secure your brand) on all the top channels. Almost all the sites offer you profile pages that you can use to add links back to your primary site and descriptive text. Some, such as Facebook, Google +, and LinkedIn, offer special business-only pages which may be appropriate for your company.

One useful tool to jumpstart profile creation is KnowEm, (`http://knowem.com`), which will search hundreds of the most popular social sites to check the availability of your preferred username. You can then either follow the link they provide and set up your account, or for a small fee, have KnowEm do it for you.

Reporting and tracking

By definition, SEO is an on-going process. One of the keys to attaining continuous improvement is tracking your efforts. While it does take time to monitor and track, the good news is that there are some great free tools to help you with this.

The most important tool in your SEO tracking toolbox is your web traffic analysis program. Google Analytics is a great choice for filling this role, as it is both free and full-featured. In the final portion of this chapter, we look at the key data points provided by Google Analytics and how that information can help you refine and improve your on-going SEO efforts.

You will also want to look at other, more specific tools, for example, social media tracking tools that help you judge the success of your engagement efforts. There are a number of tools designed to provide feedback on your SMO efforts; which you choose will largely depend on which channels you are using for your social media marketing.

Popularity metrics

Popularity metrics are yardsticks by which you can judge the relative popularity of your content over time. The primary metrics are:

- Unique visitors
- Visits
- Page views (impressions)
- Average visit length

Let's take a quick look at each of these popularity metrics.

The number of unique visitors is perhaps the most vital statistic, as it counts the visitors to your site while factoring out double counting. Be aware that there are limitations to the counting. The primary impact comes from what are known as "masked IP addresses" that is, networks that automatically give all their users the same IP address. This brings us to an important point: unique visitors does not count people; it counts computers, and that is the root of the problem. If, for example, two members of a family use the same computer to visit your site one week, you only see one visitor in the number of unique visitors' stats.

The visits statistic, on the other hand, gives the total number of visits to your website during the reporting period. It is a useful metric that will help you arrive at a meaningful conclusion regarding the activity trends on your site. Using both unique visitors and visits, you can run a quick visits per visitor calculation as a means of assessing repeat visitors.

 Many analytics programs, including Google Analytics, automatically split out repeat visitors and new visitors in the analytics dashboard.

Page views (also called impressions) tells you the total number of pages viewed by site visitors during the reporting period. If visitor A looks at just the home page, but visitor B explores the site, visiting nine pages before leaving, visitors A and B would be collectively responsible for 10 page views. Here again, you will want to look at the average number of page views per visitor. Tracking the trend in this statistic gives you a way of assessing how effective your content is at engaging visitors.

Forget about "hits." While the term is often used, the metric is of little practical use. Hits simply tells you the number of requests for files received by the server. While this may initially sound good, it falls apart when you consider that a single web page can contain a large number of individual files, each of which is counted and contributes to the total hit count. Unique visitors, views, and page views are much more useful metrics.

The final primary popularity metric is average visit length. Ever wondered if your site is sticky? This statistic and the average pages per visit stat give you a good idea how sticky your site is. Track this metric across time to assess trend. Content-heavy sites, subscription sites, and sites relying on ad revenues, obsess on this number as it indicates pretty clearly the success of their efforts to draw and hold an audience.

Traffic source metrics

Where are your visitors coming from? What keywords are bringing them to the site? Look to your analytics reports for answers to these questions. Your Google Analytics dashboard will tell you the sources of traffic, be it search engines or referrals, or even e-mail. Look carefully at the various sources driving traffic.

The search engines section of the analytics reports will also tell you which keyphrases are driving traffic. Look not only at the number of visitors produced by each keyphrase but also at the amount of time those visitors spend on the site and the number of pages they viewed; this gives you good insight into whether your content is matching up well with your keyphrase strategy.

Look at the geographic information in your analytics to assess your progress in your target markets and to discover new markets.

The referring sites information can be a good source of potential leads for link building.

e-Business metrics

Measuring the success of your website in terms that are meaningful to management means looking for those metrics that are directly relevant to the site's business goals; what we'll call e-business metrics. This is not a fixed set of indicators common to all sites, but rather a set of indicators that vary according to the nature of the business, its online presence, and the firm's business goals.

There is some common ground here with the popularity metrics discussed previously. The amount of time visitors stay on your site is clearly relevant to whether your site is effective at delivering its message. Of course, this still needs to be tied back to your goals and target markets, and you must take a look at where they are spending the time. In other words, determining the significance of this metric is more involved than simply crunching numbers.

If your firm is concerned with selling advertising space, page views is a key metric for you, as each new page gives you a chance for further ad impressions, which correlates directly to ad revenues.

Conversion rates are a common measure of a business's ability to inspire prospects to take action. While the most common focus is on purchases, conversion rates should not be so narrowly defined. Conversion can also mean registration for a newsletter, download of a product brochure, even participation in a discussion board.

Benchmarking conversion across the site requires you to look at a variety of numbers to get the full picture. For example, if your site provides an option to become a member or sign up for a newsletter, your analytics may not give you the clearest picture. Instead, you should count the number of new registrations actually received.

Google Analytics allows you to set up "goals" and "funnels," which put a special emphasis on the users' completion of certain actions, whether it is looking at a page, submitting a form, or placing an order. You can also set values to each goal, allowing you to more easily measure ROI. When creating goals, make sure you mark the end of the process (often a "thank you" or confirmation page), not the beginning or an interim step, else your data will fail to take into account abandonment—that is, people who begin the process but fail to complete it successfully.

Sites focused on online sales should, of course, be tracking the conversion rates as they relate to purchases, but there are also a number of other stats of interest. In addition to the number of purchases, you should at least be tracking the items per purchase and the value of purchases. Some firms engage in very granular analysis of e-commerce performance and if you wish to really dig into these metrics you will need tools that allow you to slice and dice the data accumulated in your database for each transaction.

Another valuable indicator of e-commerce success is shopping cart abandonment, that is, how many people put items into their shopping cart but then failed to make a purchase. This number should be tracked across time and consistent efforts must be made to manage this number. A high percentage of abandoned transactions may signal problems with the site's usability or technical glitches that require your attention.

In contrast, if you are not selling online but only marketing your company for offline sales, a key metric for e-business success is leads generated for your sales team. While it is easy to track the number of inquiry e-mails or forms you may receive from your site, it is an incomplete metric. Many people will prefer to contact you directly, rather than submit an online inquiry. In order to track this, your intake process (regardless of the channel used) for prospects should include questions about how the prospect found your firm.

In the end, the relevance of particular metrics will vary from firm to firm and you will have to make a decision about what to look at, how often, and how much weight to give it. Data is not the goal, but rather intelligence.

Link metrics

To track your success gathering inbound links, you will need to look beyond Google Analytics. There are several tools you can use, including your Google and Bing Webmaster accounts. While Google and Bing are free and easy to use (assuming you've already set up the accounts, as we advised in earlier chapters), there is a much better solution: Majestic SEO.

Majestic SEO provides both a free and a premium subscription service. If you control the site you want to track, and have access to the site's root directory on the server, then you can use the free service. Once you have registered, and verified your ownership of the site, you can use Majestic SEO to produce rich reports on the link history of the site. The data is very complete, and allows you to track both internal and external links, to view trend over time, and to look at a variety of other metrics. Visit http://www.majesticseo.com and register to get started.

 Alexa.com also provides a basic link count, but no data on trend, target, or anchor text.

Summary

This chapter focused on the ongoing work required to conduct an effective, sustained SEO campaign. The key point made in this chapter is that you need to maintain your SEO efforts throughout the life of your site through a combination of techniques.

We looked specifically at link building and social media optimization. Link building was discussed in detail, with an emphasis on how to identify potential link partners and then create and manage a link building campaign. A number of the leading sites were identified in a variety of areas.

Social media's increasing role in search marketing was also highlighted, with a recommendation made to not only be proactive about using social media to promote your content but also to inspire and motivate your users to promote your content through their social networks.

In the final part of this chapter we discussed the importance of monitoring your progress and feeding the data back into your efforts in order to attain continuous refinement and improvement in your SEO efforts. The emphasis was on how to use the key metrics you can find in Google Analytics, but the information is relevant to any web traffic monitoring program.

Index

Googlebot 18
Google Hot Trends page 59
Google Webmaster Tools
  about 12, 72, 73
  URL 73

H

H2 tag 68
Hackernews
  URL 87
hits 90
H tag 68
HTTP traffic 9

I

img tag 10
i-Newswire
  URL 84
installing
  SEO modules 43
internal link density 12
Issuu
  URL 86

J

Joomla! 6

K

KEI 12, 62
keyphrase. *See* keyword
keyphrase density 13
Keyphrase Effectiveness Index. *See* KEI
keyphrase stuffing 13
keyword density 67
keyword effectiveness
  assessing 62-64
keyword
  about 13, 60
  effectiveness, assessing 62-64
  identifying 56-61
KnowEm
  about 88
  URL 88

L

landing page 13
Larry Page 15
link bait 82
link building
  about 13, 77
  link marketing campaign, managing 81, 82
  quality link partners, identifying 79, 80
Link Building Query Generator 80
LinkDetective
  URL 79
LinkedIn
  about 88
  URL 87
link farm 13
link marketing campaign
  managing 81, 82
link metrics 92
links
  categories 78
  creating 83
links, categories
  organic 78
  self-created 78
  solicited 78
link text 14
live site
  SEO, managing on 77
long tail
  about 14
  advantages 61

M

menu items
  title attribute, controlling 33
Metacafe
  URL 85
metadata
  about 14, 69
  managing 69, 70
metadata management
  implementing 46, 47
meta tags 14

Meta Tags module
  about 40, 46
  setting up 46, 47
  URL 40
MozRank
  about 14
  URL 80
MozTrust
  URL 80

N

Newsvine
  URL 87
nofollow 14, 78

O

Ontolo
  about 82
  URL 82
Open Site Explorer
  URL 79
organic links 78
organic rank 14
outbound link 14

P

Page Not Found. *See* **404 error**
PageRank 14, 15, 80
Page ranking indicators 84
Page Title module
  about 40
  setting up 47
  URL 40
page views 89
Pathauto module
  about 40, 44
  setting up 44
  URL 40
Path module
  about 29
  enabling 29
Pay Per Click. *See* **PPC**
Permanent Redirect. *See* **301 redirect**
Photobucket
  URL 85

photo sharing 85
photo sharing sites
  about 85
  Flickr 85
  Photobucket 85
  Picasa 85
  Pinterest 85
  SmugMug 85
phrases
  identifying 56-61
Picasa
  URL 85
Pinterest
  URL 85
popularity metrics 89
PPC 15
press release distribution services
  Free Press Release 84
  i-Newswire 84
  PRinside 84
  PRLog 84
press releases 84
PRinside
  URL 84
PRLeap
  URL 85
PRLog
  URL 84
PRWeb
  URL 85

Q

quality directories
  identifying 84
quality link partners
  identifying 79, 80

R

reciprocal link 15
Reddit
  URL 87
redirect 15
rel attribute 14
relevancy 66

T

TagClouds module
  about 43
  URL 43
tagging 31
taxonomy
  about 31
  setting up 31-33
Technorati 88
Temporary Redirect or Found.
    See **302 redirect**
terms
  adding, to vocabulary 32
third-party services
  Bing Webmaster Tools 74
  Google Analytics 71, 72
  Google Webmaster Tools 72, 73
  setting up 71
title attribute 16, 33
Title Tag management
  implementing 47
traffic source metrics 90
Trellian KW Discovery tool
  URL 60
trends
  targeting 59
Twitter
  about 59
  URL 87
Twitter Trends 59

U

Ubersuggest
  URL 60

V

variants 65
Veoh
  URL 85

video and file sharing sites
  about 85
  Dailymotion 85
  Metacafe 85
  Photobucket 85
  Veoh 85
  Vimeo 85
Vimeo
  URL 85
vocabulary
  about 30
  creating 31
  terms, adding to 32

W

web.config file 9
website discovery tool
  using 57
WebWire
  URL 85
White hat 17
WordStream
  URL 60
Wordtracker
  URL 60

X

XML sitemap
  about 17, 43, 50
  setting up 50
  URL 43

Y

Yahoo! Directory
  URL 83

Thank you for buying
Drupal Search Engine Optimization

About Packt Publishing

Packt, pronounced 'packed', published its first book *"Mastering phpMyAdmin for Effective MySQL Management"* in April 2004 and subsequently continued to specialize in publishing highly focused books on specific technologies and solutions.

Our books and publications share the experiences of your fellow IT professionals in adapting and customizing today's systems, applications, and frameworks. Our solution based books give you the knowledge and power to customize the software and technologies you're using to get the job done. Packt books are more specific and less general than the IT books you have seen in the past. Our unique business model allows us to bring you more focused information, giving you more of what you need to know, and less of what you don't.

Packt is a modern, yet unique publishing company, which focuses on producing quality, cutting-edge books for communities of developers, administrators, and newbies alike. For more information, please visit our website: www.packtpub.com.

About Packt Open Source

In 2010, Packt launched two new brands, Packt Open Source and Packt Enterprise, in order to continue its focus on specialization. This book is part of the Packt Open Source brand, home to books published on software built around Open Source licenses, and offering information to anybody from advanced developers to budding web designers. The Open Source brand also runs Packt's Open Source Royalty Scheme, by which Packt gives a royalty to each Open Source project about whose software a book is sold.

Writing for Packt

We welcome all inquiries from people who are interested in authoring. Book proposals should be sent to author@packtpub.com. If your book idea is still at an early stage and you would like to discuss it first before writing a formal book proposal, contact us; one of our commissioning editors will get in touch with you.

We're not just looking for published authors; if you have strong technical skills but no writing experience, our experienced editors can help you develop a writing career, or simply get some additional reward for your expertise.

Drupal 7 Themes

ISBN: 978-1-84951-276-3   Paperback: 320 pages

Create new themes for your Drupal 7 site with a clean layout and powerful CSS styling

1. Learn to create new Drupal 7 themes

2. No experience of Drupal theming required

3. Discover techniques and tools for creating and modifying themes

4. The first book to guide you through the new elements and themes available in Drupal 7

Drupal 7

ISBN: 978-1-84951-286-2   Paperback: 416 pages

Create and operate any type of website quickly and efficiently

1. Set up, configure, and deploy a Drupal 7 website

2. Easily add exciting and powerful features

3. Design and implement your website's look and feel

4. Promote, manage, and maintain your live website

5. In-depth coverage of Drupal's new core features, including image handling and fields

Please check **www.PacktPub.com** for information on our titles

Drupal 7 Module Development

ISBN: 978-1-84951-116-2   Paperback: 420 pages

Create your own Drupal 7 modules from scratchs

1. Specifically written for Drupal 7 development

2. Write your own Drupal modules, themes, and libraries

3. Discover the powerful new tools introduced in Drupal 7

4. Learn the programming secrets of six experienced Drupal developers

5. Get practical with this book's project-based format

Drupal 7 Cookbook

ISBN: 978-1-84951-796-6   Paperback: 324 pages

Over 70 recipes that will advance your Drupal skills from novice to pro

1. Install, set up, and manage a Drupal site and discover how to get the most out of creating and displaying content

2. Become familiar with creating new content types and use them to create and publish content using Views, Blocks, and Panels

3. Learn how to work with images, documents, and video and how to integrate them with Facebook, Twitter, and Add this